ACOUSTIC GUITAR

FOR BEGINNERS

The Ultimate Beginner's Guide to Learn the Realms of Acoustic Guitar from A-Z

PETER F. SHELDON

Table of Contents

Introduction

As a beginner, one of the most recommendable types of guitar to start with is the acoustic guitar. An acoustic guitar is characterized by the presence of a sound box, which amplifies the sound of the strings. With an acoustic guitar, you don't need an amplifier or speakers to produce a solid sound. As such, you can easily pick up an acoustic guitar and practice anywhere. Acoustic guitars produce a soulful and beautiful sound, making it quite a versatile instrument usable in so many music genres. So, wanting to learn how to play an acoustic guitar might just be one of the coolest instruments you will learn this year.

As we know it, the guitar is about a century old or older, and the root as a stringed instrument goes deep into history. For thousands of years many folk instruments followed the same basic design of strings stretched over the fretboard and plucked with the fingers. In a way, the guitar is the culmination of that legacy, hence the guitar's versatility. As long as you're a guitar lover, you'd find this book quite useful. No matter your experience, situation, or motives, the goal of this book is to provide you with enough information so that you can explore everything on your own.

It is common for beginners to feel as though they are stuck at a certain point in their guitar learning. With this beginner's guide, we will enlighten you with exceptional methods that will skyrocket your learning curve. Understanding what you can do with the guitar, finding new ways to make new sounds, and a better grasp of how to fret notes and chords that seemed impossible before becomes tremendously exciting and satisfying. All these await you as long as you are willing to put in some time and effort to understand everything this book entails.

We don't assume you know anything about playing a guitar or reading music. So, for you to understand everything about playing the guitar from scratch. We start this guide from the basics to make comprehension easier. And with the straightforward, informal explanation of how guitars work, the different types of guitar, and how you can play, form chords, strum, and fingerpick strings, you can overall deepen your knowledge in so many directions. Without any further introduction, let us start with guitar history and work our way to something more advanced.

Chapter 1

History and Types of Guitar

To start this beginner's guide on how to play an acoustic guitar, let us take a little detour to the history of guitars. We find this particularly important to discuss it first because it is always best to know where it all began. Guitars are widely played in so many countries, folk and popular music, which resulted in the multiple origin stories we all hear when we ask where the guitar was born.

Depending on who you ask, the story of the guitar's birth stretches from Persia to Greece. Perhaps it was born in all this region, but in variations of strings, plucked instruments found worldwide, indicating the ingenuity and creativity that transcends culture.

History of the Guitar

The guitar is a string instrument that originated from Spain in the early 16th century. What we now know as the guitar is an instrument derived from the late-medieval instrument, Guitarra Latina. The Guitarra Latina is a four-string instrument. The earliest forms of guitars had a less pronounced waist, narrower and deeper than the guitars we see today. Guitarra Latina is in a lot of aspects related to the Vihuela. Vihuela is an instrument shaped like a guitar that is mainly played in Spain instead of the Lute. Earlier guitars had only four strings; three doubles and a single top string. The strings were glued and stretched from the tension bridge to the soundboard or belly of the guitar, like in the case of the violin peg-box. The bridge sustains the direct pull of the strings. You will also find a circular sound hole in the guitar's belly, often ornamented with a carved wooden rose.

Most of the improvements we see on the guitar today were made between the 16th and 19th centuries. In the 16th century, the four strings of guitars were tuned to sound C-F-A-D apart, like tuning the center four courses of the Vihuela and the Lute. Before 1600, a 5th string was added to the guitar, and in the late 18th century, the 6th string was added. Around the year 1800, music inventors replaced the guitar's double strings with a single string, making the guitar tune to E-A-D-G-B-E, which to date remained the standard for tuning the guitar.

Another improvement done on the guitar was sometime in 1600 when the violin-styled peg-box was replaced with a flat and slightly reflexed head with rear tuning pegs. Later on, in the 19th century, inventors came up with metal screws in place of the tuning pegs. Previously, the frets were tied to the guitar's gut, but it was later replaced with ivory or metal fret in the 18th century. Originally, the fingerboard was flush with the belly and ended there, with some ivory or metal frets on the belly. Later in the 19th century, more development was done on the fingerboard, raising it to a level higher than the belly, causing it to extend across the edge of the sound hole.

Additionally, in the 19th century, the guitar's body went through a couple of changes, which increased the instrument's sonority. This improvement caused the guitar to become broader and shallower with an extremely thin soundboard. Likewise, the transverse bars that internally reinforce the soundboard were replaced with radial bars fanning out below the sound hole. Also, the guitar's neck forms a brace or shoe, which projects a short distance inside the body of the guitar, and it is glued to the back. This development gave the guitar extra stability against the pull of the string.

So, it's no doubt that the guitar or the instruments related to the guitar have existed since ancient times. The idea of a stretched string vibrating over a chamber of air called the sound box is not a new idea. This idea dates back to prehistoric times founded in so many cultures in the world. The use of frets to mark the tones to scale the sound most likely originated in India. Later on, early explorers from Portugal and Spain probably brought the idea of the guitar to Europe, and European settlers brought it to America.

Antonio Torres, the most important Spanish guitar maker, was the brain behind most of the innovations seen on the guitar in the 19th century. Most acoustic guitars seen today were a derivative of his design. Even the classical guitar strung with three metal-spun silk and three gut strings resulted from his design. Later on, as things improved, manufacturers started using plastic and nylon strings in place of the gut. Among the different variants of guitars, the 12 stringed or double course guitar, Mexican Jarana, and South America Charango (both of which are five-course guitars) were strung with nylon or plastic strings. In the 19th century, the Lyre-shaped guitars were the most fashionable. But other forms of guitar, including the metal, strung guitars played with a plectrum in folk and popular music, the cello guitar with a tailpiece, and violin-styled bridge. Other forms of guitars include the Hawaiian or steel-strung guitar with its strings stopped by the pressure of a metal bar, which produces a sweet gliding tone, and lastly, we have the electric guitar.

Types of Guitar

Today there are so many types of guitars; it almost feels impossible to keep up with the trend. What is even more frustrating is that acoustic guitar can look very similar. And acoustic guitars are made with wood, so they all have a sound hole, and they all have strings, so there is no obvious distinguishing feature. But mainly, guitars are classified based on the types of strings they use, body shape, and tone wood design. So, to help you understand better, below is an outline of the different types of acoustic guitars and what genre to use them for as well as some features you'll find useful.

1. *Dreadnought Guitar*

Dreadnought guitar is a very popular type of guitar you can find in the market today. Out of the various types of guitar available today, the dreadnought guitar still remains the most affordable. They were developed in the 20th century by the American guitar manufacturer C.F. Martin & Company. The name dreadnought guitar originates from the large, all-big-gun modern battleship HMS Dreadnought. It has a large body, which provides you with a bolder, louder, and richer tone. A distinguishing feature of the dreadnought guitar is its size, square shoulder, and bottom. Also, the neck of dreadnought guitars is usually attached to the body at the fourteenth fret.

Another name for C.F. Martin & Company dreadnought guitar is the D-sized guitar or simply referred to as dreads amongst guitarists. The model number of C.F. Martin & Company dreadnought guitar starts with a D followed by a number, like D-18 or D-45. Note, the higher the number assigned to the model number, the more the decoration and ornamentation on the guitar. Dreadnought guitars are great for aggressive strummers and flat pickers, especially those who want a strong but a cheap guitar. Blues guitarists commonly use dreadnought guitars.

2. Jumbo Guitar

The jumbo guitar is another common type of guitar amongst guitarists popularized by Gibson in the 1930s. Compared to the dreadnought guitar, the jumbo guitar has a more curved centric design. Jumbo guitars are characterized by their relatively big sound box producing the most air inside the body, which means more energy coming out of them. Jumbo guitars usually have a circular style body with a tight-waist that gives it a top-end snap and presence. Because of its tighter waist, the jumbo guitar doesn't lose clarity or sound muddy.

Note, the jumbo guitar is not best for fingerpicking players or players with a gentle approach, but it is the ultimate strummer's guitar. Jumbo guitars are often used in big folk, pop, and country songs. Moreover, the tonal spectrum of the jumbo acoustic guitar is balanced. From personal experience, I can tell you that the larger cavity produces a more open type of sound that can accentuate the bass frequencies. Famous guitarists like George Harrison, Elvis, etc. play the Jumbo guitar.

3. Parlor Guitar

On the other end of the shape sits this parlor acoustic guitar. This guitar is among the smallest in body size of guitar you can buy – not counting modern baby guitars available today. Parlor guitars are favored by players with a more low-key, less brash musical style like indie and folk. Once again, this guitar's distinctive body shape is from C.F Martin & Company, with its neck joined to the body on the 12th fret.

The shoulder where the body joins with the neck is sloped slightly more than you'd see in dreadnought acoustic guitars. While at the same time, the base of a guitar's body will be narrower than a larger sized guitar. And in the end, the target is to make it more comfortable to play and create a less physically challenging playing experience. In terms of precedent, parlor guitars are associated with the renowned guitarist Ian Anderson.

4. *Rounded Shoulders Dreadnought Guitar*

After considering the three main shapes of steel stung acoustic guitar – talking about the dreadnought, jumbo, and parlor guitar, let us take our time to check out the off-shoots and variants. First amongst this category is the rounded shoulder dreadnought guitar. This guitar is a well-known and identifiable Gibson creation famously employed by Noel Gallagher and the Beatles. It is hard to overlook the rounded shoulder dreadnought guitar because of its sweet, warm, and beautifully sounding high notes defined in the mid-range.

The origin of the rounded shoulder dreadnought guitar is from the replication of Martin's dreadnought guitar. Gibson created a slight variant to the dreadnought, which later became extremely popular. After its popularity surged, it was known as a "workhorse" guitar, affordable yet easier to maintain than the more expensive dreadnought. The price of the rounded shoulders dreadnought contributed to the rise to prominence and its warm tone that offer a luscious sound that complements any vocalist creating that sensation acoustic arena.

5. Auditorium Guitars

Auditorium guitars are similar to the dreadnought guitar, but they have a more recent developmental history. Once again, this type of guitar is from the C.F. Martin house designs. While this guitar offers you a similar dimension to the dreadnought guitar. But a closer look at the auditorium guitar reveals that it comes with a much tighter waist, which can cause certain tonal characteristics to become a lot more pronounced. Based on the design, the auditorium guitar fits over your leg snugger because of its refined waist.

On the auditorium guitar, the body's inner curves have been defined more inward, which decreases the amount of inner cavity of the guitar shape. This feature is particularly a plus for players who love to have their guitar sit firmly on their legs without any tendency to move around. A famous guitarist associated with playing the auditorium guitar in his repertoire is no other than Eric Clapton. If you have heard his "unplugged" album, you will be familiar with the beautiful tones that can evolve from the auditorium guitar.

6. Concert Guitar

The concert guitar is another type of acoustic guitar, distinct both in tone and functionality. Overall, concert guitars sound more pleasing and playable. Apart from that, concert guitars are small compared to other more robust guitars like dreadnought guitars. Even though concert guitars lack the volume, manufacturers make up for it with articulating tones that are stronger in the upper and middle ranges. Take note, the size and shape of a guitar not only affect the sound but also how it plays. As such, the small compact nature of concert guitars feels very comfortable for smaller people to play.

Guitarists who love the sound of fingerpicking will appreciate the concert guitar more because of their lower string tension. Morcover, the articulate tone of concert guitars gives them an advantage for fingerpicking. Remember, there are no hard and fast rules stating who should and shouldn't play the concert guitar. So, if you love the positive features of the guitar, then let nothing hold you back.

7. *Classical Guitar*

Classical guitar is another type of guide known for its soft nylon-string tone, although you can also string them with a steel string and enjoy the unique sound of steel strings. One of the easiest ways to identify a classical guitar is from their open slotted tuners. The slotted tuners make use of cams and not standard tuning posts. The tuner knobs often recede in a perpendicular direction from the back of the headstock rather than parallel with the headstock's side. A common example of a classical guitar is the all famous Spanish guitar.

If you are a lover of fingerpicking or soft sounds, especially from the European orchestral music, then the classical guitar is a worthy investment. Similarly, if you are a lover of strumming, the classical guitars can easily become a bright strummer. Famous guitarists associated with the classical guitar include the likes of Willie Nelson and Andres Segovia to Christopher Parkening.

8. Travel Guitar

As the name implies, travel guitars are suitable for players who travel a lot or with small hands. Parents frequently shop for this type of guitar for their children because of its extremely compact design. This guitar was designed to provide comfort for a small player and convenience while traveling. One of the major problems with smaller guitars is that it compromises on sound quality. As such, music manufacturers put in a lot of time and resources into creating the perfect small-scale acoustic guitar; thus, the travel guitar emerged.

While they may be small and cute, they are not considered toys; most of them feature a full-size fretboard, or a close to a full-sized fretboard of length around 23 inches and provide a very similar playing experience to a full-sized guitar. In some cases, they may even cost more than a standard acoustic guitar. Most travel guitars are made of laminated wood to ensure they are resistant to humidity and temperature and are lightweight.

9. Flamenco Guitar

Finally, the flamenco guitar is another type of guitar similar to the classical guitar, but they have a thinner top and less internal bracing. Flamenco guitar produces a brighter and percussive sound quality due to its thinner top. Most flamenco guitars use nylon strings instead of steel strings, which gives them that livelier sound compared to classical guitars. The volume of flamenco guitar has been very important to guitarists because it is heard over the sound of the dancers' nailed shoes. Guitar manufacturers mainly use hardwoods such as rosewood for the back and sides and softer woods for the top while constructing the flamenco guitar.

It is noteworthy that a well-constructed flamenco guitar responds quicker and has less sustenance than classical guitars. Flamenco guitars are desirable for this feature because the fury of notes that a good flamenco player can produce might sound a bit muddy on the guitar with a lush, sustained, big sound. Additionally, flamenco guitars are often described as percussive, and they tend to be drier, brighter, and more austere.

Chapter 2

Guitar Anatomy

In addition to everything covered in the first chapter, our focus in this chapter is to introduce you to the guitar in a more specific way. In this chapter, we will be considering the different parts of the guitar and the function they serve. By the end of this chapter, you will know the names of each guitar part, so that in our next chapter, when we discuss how to buy a guitar, you won get confused.

The Anatomy of a Guitar

Well, there are two basic types of guitar: electric and acoustic. Under each of these basic types of guitar, we have several subdivisions. Since our focus in this book is on the acoustic guitar, our focus will stay on the various components that make up an acoustic guitar. Generally, according to guitar manufacturers, making an electric guitar is easier than making an acoustic guitar. As such, price-wise, the acoustic guitar is often more expensive. To put an acoustic guitar together, a lot of precision needs to be put in place, especially with the sound box.

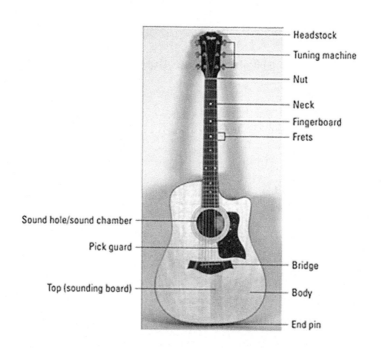

Headstock
Tuning machine
Nut
Neck
Fingerboard
Frets

Sound hole/sound chamber
Pick guard
Top (sounding board)
Bridge
Body
End pin

Look at the picture above; you can see that the acoustic guitar can be divided into three main sections - the headstock, neck, and body. On these sections of the guitar, you'll find various parts of the guitar that work together to produce a beautiful sound.

1. Headstock

The headstock is where the mechanism fastens the strings to the head of the guitar. On the headstock are the tuners. Often, the headstock is where many manufacturers inscribe their logo. There are two traditional designs of the headstock available on the market. Guitars come with a choice of two configurations - 3+3, which is 3 tuners on top and 3 at the bottom - or a 6 configuration with 6 tuners on top of the headstock. Additionally, your guitar's headstock may be straight or carved separately and glued to the neck of the guitar.

- *Tuners*

One of the essential parts of a guitar is the tuner, also known as the tuning machine, tuning keys, tuning gears, or tuning pegs. A guitar's tuner is usually found on the headstock of any guitar, both acoustic and electric. The tuners are a geared mechanism responsible for tuning the guitar. You tune a guitar using the tuners by either rotating the tuners or wrapping the string around the tuner's post. Depending on the direction you decide to rotate the tuner, you may either be tightening the strings or loosening it. Note, the tighter the tension of the string, the higher the pitch of the string.

- *Nut*

The nut is like a bridge between the headstock of the guitar and the neck of the guitar. The nut has grooves on it, which serve as a demarcation, separating the strings from each other as you tighten the strings to pitch. The nut can be made from different materials like stiff nylon, silver, bone, brass, or other synthetic substances. So, when the strings vibrate, the nut prevents the strings from vibrating beyond the neck. The nut is one of the two points on the guitar in which the vibrating area of the string ends; the other area is the bridge located on the body of the guitar.

2. Neck

A guitar's neck is the club-like, long section of the guitar connecting the body and the headstock. Most times, the neck of guitars is constructed with hardwood. The same wood is often used in constructing the fingerboard and fret while a different wood is used in constructing the neck. The neck of a guitar needs to be rigid and resistant to bending, even from high tension strings. You can determine the quality of a guitar with the rigidity of the guitar's neck. Note that the guitar's neck is an integral part of the guitar where the fingerboard and frets are located. This is where you hold the strings at different sections of the fingerboards to vary the pitch of the strings and produce a beautiful sound.

- *Fingerboard*

The fingerboard is something referred to as the fretboard because the frets are embedded in it. The fingerboard is a plank-like piece of wood often laminated, and it sits on the neck of the guitar. It is an important part of the guitar because it is where you place your finger. The strings usually run over the fingerboard between the bridge and nut. When you play the guitar, every time you depress the string on the fingerboard, you change the string's length, thus changing the pitch. You can even play notes with the fretting hands only by hammering on the string.

- *Frets*

The frets are located on the fingerboard of every guitar. The frets can be a wire or a thin bar that runs perpendicular to the strings. The frets extend over the full width of the neck at the varying distance between each fret. The closer you get to the body, the shorter the distance between the frets. Additionally, the fretboard is responsible for cutting short the string's vibrating length, enabling you to produce different pitches. Note, each fret on the guitar represents a semitone in the standard western system, where an octave is divided into twelve semitones.

- ### *Position Marker*

Position markers are in-lay single or double dot placed on the fretboard or the edge of the guitars' neck to make fret navigation easier. As a beginner learning how to play the guitar, you don't always have to count the frets to know how many you are playing on. The single dot position markers are often placed on the 3rd, 5th, 7th, and 9th frets of the guitar. And to indicate an octave higher double dots, position markers are placed high above the neck on the 12th and 24th frets. This position marker can be made illumined with light diodes to make it more visible during a stage performance.

3. Body

Moving forward, the body of the guitar is the big box on a guitar. The body provides an anchor for the neck and bridge and creates a playing surface for your right hand to strum over the strings. The body includes the amplifying sound chamber that makes the guitar produce a more pronounced tone. The body is that curvy bit of the guitar that rests against your body when playing. Take note, the guitar's body may come in different shapes. Some guitars feature a cut out near the neck, making it easy to reach the frets above the neck.

- ### *Sound Hole*

The round opening you see on the body of guitars is the sound hole. When strings vibrate over the sound hole, it amplifies the sound. On some acoustic guitars, the sound hole is usually oval in shape.

Although the sound hole amplifies and makes the sound on acoustic guitar sound better, that does not mean the sound comes solely from the sound hole. Sounds are also generated on the surface of the sounding boards. The sound hole only provides an opening into the resonant chamber formed by the body.

- ***Pickguard***

Another part of the guitar you'll find on the body is the pickguard. The pickguard does not in any way contribute to the sound of the guitar. However, the pickguard protects the finishing of your guitar from scratches. While playing the guitar, the pick won't scratch the guitar's finish if the pickguard is in place. The pickguard is made from plastic or other material, often laminated. Another function the pickguard serves is for decoration, as it is often made of a contrasting color to the color of the guitar body. High-end guitars may have luxury pick guards made from furs, exotic woods, gems, skins, or precious metal.

- ***Bridge***

The bridge of a guitar is that part of the body that supports the strings. So, the string runs from the bridge to the tuner on the headstock of any guitar. Typically, the guitars' bridge is placed perpendicular to the strings on the body and glued securely such that it can support the tension of the strings. To sustain such tension, the bridge is often constructed with high-density plastic, metal, ivory, or bone. The bridge consists of multiple parts like the bridge pin and a separate bearing surface called the saddle.

- ***Bridge Pin***

The bridge pin, sometimes called the string pegs, are used to hold the string in place. Most acoustic guitars that make use of steel strings use bridge pins. Guitar bridge pins can be made with brass, bone, ivory, wood, or even plastic. Note, not all acoustic guitars use bridge pins; it solely depends on the bridge's design. Some guitar manufacturers designed the bridge of their guitar in a way that when it comes to fastening strings, you simply pass it through the holes on the bridge, and the string ball at the end of the string holds the string in place from going through the bridge's hole.

- ***Saddle***

The saddle is also another part of the guitar found on the bridge of the guitar. The saddle has an impact on the overall height of the strings over the fretboard. The closer the strings are to the fretboard, the easier the strings will be on your left hands when holding chords. So, the saddle has a larger influence on the guitar's playability and tone than you think. Saddles come in two different kinds, compensated and uncompensated saddles. Compensated saddles include notches or grooves where the high E, B, and G strings rest. As such, this adjusts the length of the string, compensating for accurate intonation. On the other hand, the uncompensated saddle does not come with any grooves as it is flat across the surface.

- ***End Pin***

The endpin is a metal post at the rear end of the guitar body where you can connect the guitar's strap. In some acoustic-electric guitars with built-in electronics and pickups, the pin contains the output hack for routing signals from the guitar's preamp and pickup.

4. Strings

The last one is the string; it is a vital part of the guitar responsible for actually producing the sound. When plunked, the strings vibrate, which produces sounds that are amplified in the sound box. The string of a guitar stretches from the bridge to the tuner on the headstock. You can use different kinds of strings on your guitar to give you the sound you desire. The two common types of strings are the nylon string and metal string.

How A Guitar Works

Now that we have established the basic parts of the guitar, our next target is to understand how they all work together to make a sound. Our main focus in this section will be to learn how the guitar works. We will be addressing topics like the strings, plucking the strings, and how the frets affect the sound you make.

1. String Vibration and String Length

The guitar produces sound as a result of vibrating strings over a sound box. As we have established in the previous chapter, there are basically six strings on an acoustic guitar. But these strings need to be brought to a certain tension. A tuned string is so named after the note it produces when it is plucked open. So, the A string is named the A string because playing the A string opened produces an A note. But when you change the string's length by fretting it, you can change the note. Hence, by varying the length of the strings, you can produce something melodious.

2. *Playing with Your Left and Right Hand*

Like we just established above, you need your left hand fretting the string, and your right hand plucking the string to play the guitar. When you hold a note or a chord with your left hand on a guitar, your right hand is responsible for plucking or strumming the string to produce the sound of the note or chord you are holding. Later in this book, we will talk extensively on playing notes and chords on the guitar.

3. *A Fret is a Half-Step*

Moving from one fret to another on the guitar is a half-step. So, you have to move two frets on the guitar to move a whole step. So, rather than the 6 frets, you need to move 12 frets to play an octave on the guitar.

4. *Pickups*

The sound from a vibrating string needs to be amplified; else, it won't be loud enough. With the acoustic guitar, you have no problem, as the hollow sound chamber amplifies the sound.

How a guitar sounds different from the sound you have in mind depends on how you control the pitches. Your left hand is for fretting, which you'll use to change the pitches, while the right-hand motion helps produce the sound and determines the rhythm, tempo, and feel of those pitches. So, putting both hands to action spells the guitar music.

Counting Your Strings and Frets

One of the biggest challenges of getting started with playing any musical instruments is getting to understand the instrument intensely. This painstaking process of tuning the guitar can be quite challenging. Fortunately for guitarists, there are only six strings on a guitar as opposed to the piano. But before you start tuning the guitar, you need to know how to refer to the two main parts of the guitar – frets and strings.

1. Strings

As we mentioned earlier, there are six strings on a guitar labeled 1 through 6. The guitar's 1st string is the thinnest and the closest to the floor when holding the guitar in a playing position. Working your way up, the 6th string is the fattest string and the one closest to the ceiling when holding the guitar in a playing position. The numbering of a guitar's strings may seem counterintuitive because looking at the guitar when holding it in a playing position, the first string you see is what you may want to call the first string, but it is actually the 6th string. From the 1st to the 6th strings, the strings are labeled E, B, G, D, A, and E.

2. Frets

The frets should also be labeled as they indicate the spaces where you place your left-hand fingers to vary the strings' length to change the pitch of the guitar. The 1st fret is the region closest to the nut.

Similarly, the 5th fret is the region between the fourth and fifth metal bars. Many guitars have markers on the 5th fret, either a dot or a decorative design embedded in the fretboard.

Chapter 3

Buying and Stringing a Guitar

If you don't already have a guitar, well, you need to get one. In this chapter, we will enlighten you on how to get the best guitar. Keep in mind the whole process of buying a guitar; it is exciting and tantalizing. One way to know the difference between a good guitar and a great guitar is when you indulge yourself. Play a range of guitars to understand the differences between high-quality guitar, expensive guitars, and acceptable but affordable guitars.

Developing a Buying Strategy

The first thing you need to do when trying to buy a guitar is to develop a buying strategy. In this section, you need to ask yourself a series of questions and answer them with all sincerity. Remember, there are no right or wrong answers. You shouldn't wait till you are right there in the store before you start developing a buying strategy. The two most important things to note when making a buying strategy is to develop a plan and to gather all the information you need. So, ask yourself the following questions:

1. What's My Level of Commitment?

Your current playing ability aside for now, ask yourself, do you really see yourself practicing the guitar daily for the next five years?

Or do you see yourself just trying out the guitar to explore new things, and hope that it might stick? If the former is your case, then investing a lot of money to buy a high-quality guitar will go a long way. But if the latter is your case, then it wouldn't be advisable to spend too much on a guitar, well at least not until you are sure of its importance in your life. Importantly, when spending on a guitar, act responsibly, and according to your priority.

2. What is My Spending Limit?

Another very critical question you need to ask yourself is the amount you are willing to spend. The more expensive a guitar is, the more appealing the guitar. So, if you want to go by what feels appealing to you, you may end up spending more than you can afford. You must balance your level of commitment to the amount available. Set a limit on how much you can spend and don't exceed it.

3. Do I Buy Online or Buy From a Mall?

If you have everything all pictured up in your mind down to the color and options you want, then you can consider buying the guitar from an online vendor. But if you are still skeptical about the particular guitar you want to settle for, then you should go to a mall to buy one. You can even test the guitar at the mall and have a feel of it before buying it. Moreover, when buying a guitar from the mall, you can get the best deals and even avoid paying sales tax, especially when the music company is out of state.

4. *Am I a New-Guitar Person or a Used-Guitar Person?*

What kind of person are you? If you want to go for a used guitar, note that vintage instruments can be quite expensive, but they give you a different kind of feeling when you play it. But there are other less expensive used guitars you can buy if you are on a low budget. And not to mention the attributes associated with new guitars that used guitars may lack. On the other hand, if you prefer the feeling of playing a brand-new guitar and can afford to buy one, well, feel free. Look out for stores that offer discounts at different rates.

Know What You Want in a Guitar

Knowing the minimum you can afford to spend on a guitar is an important buyer's guide feature you should consider. A budget sets you in a class of products, giving you an idea of what you are likely to end up buying. For instance, an individual budgeting $1000 and another individual budgeting $200, you can't expect the individual with a $200 budget to get a more superior guitar than the individual with a $1000 budget. Your budget affects the quality you get at the end of the day. Below are a few factors affected by your budget.

1. *Appearance*

The appearance of your guitar is related to the aesthetic properties of the guitar. The nice wood finishing used and the color all come to play here. When you love the way your guitar looks, you feel very encouraged to pick it up for practice. Feel free to base your decision on the look of the guitar that you like to buy. A green guitar is not better or worse than a red guitar.

2. *Playability*

Some guitars are easier to play than others, and it is important to have this at the back of your mind when getting a guitar. Cheaper guitars are often more difficult to play because of the less workmanship put in place during construction. It is common amongst cheap guitars to have its string far from its fret. As such, you will find it relatively hard to depress the string to the fretboard.

3. *Intonation*

A quality guitar must play in tune. Playing the 12th fret harmonic (barely touch the fret rather than pressing it down) on the 1st string and matching it to the fretted note at the 12th fret is how you test the intonation of a guitar. However, the pitch may be the same, but the notes are of different tonal qualities. You can use this same test on all six strings on the guitar and carefully listen to the 3rd and 6th strings. The 3rd and 6th strings are usually the first to go out of tune.

4. *Solid Construction*

Lastly, the aspect of the type of construction used on the guitar you want to buy is determined by your budget. Keep a close eye on a well-constructed guitar by examining every joint for sloppy workmanship. A roughly sanded brace is a big tip-off that the guitar was hastily constructed.

Buying a Guitar

First, you need to decide how much you are willing to spend to start on the right foot. Having a large budget doesn't necessarily mean you will get the best guitar. There are certain features about the guitar you need to have in mind if you want to get the best. Below is a summary of everything you need to watch out for:

1. Construction

When we talk about the guitar's construction, we are referring to how it is designed and assembled. The construction of a guitar defines the guitar and the kind of music it can play with ease. Below are the three most important issues regarding the construction of the guitar.

Solid Wood vs. Laminated Wood

The quality of the guitar ranges from solid wood to laminated wood guitar. But to be honest, solid wood guitar stands a better chance at lasting longer than laminated wood guitar. Irrespective of this, most manufacturers use several layers of inexpensive wood, pressed together and veneered, which won't last that long. Guitars made with solid wood tend to be more durable, but their cost can go as high as $1000.

The type of wood you'd find on guitars is a critical element in sound production. When plucking a guitar string, its sound vibrates in the sound box, hitting the back and sides before reflecting through the sound hole. Settling for hardwood guitar is a good choice, but it helps look at various configurations like the top being solid and various parts being laminated to reduce the cost. A good choice will be a guitar with a solid top but laminated back and side, which may cost you about $400.

Body Caps

Whether the guitar you want to buy has a cap or not, it is another determining factor of the quality. This feature also reflects the price of the guitar. The cap serves as a layer of fine decorative wood; it is often of a figured maple variety. Manufacturers also make use of other popular woods like quilted and flame maple. And when manufacturers want to make a guitar with a clear finish to show off the wood's attractive grain pattern, they make use of figured wood tops.

Neck Construction

Here are the three common types of neck construction in order of their price, starting from the least to the most expensive:

- *Bolt-On*

Some guitars come with a bolt-on type of construction. In this type of guitar, the neck is attached to the guitar's back at the heel using 4 or 5 bolts. However, the heel plates may sometimes cover the holes of the bolt.

- *Set-In (or Glued-In)*

Another common construction that comes with guitars is the neck and body joined in an unbroken surface covering connection. This construction type provides a seamless effect from the body to the neck, and the joints are glued together.

- *Neck-Through Body*

This is another common type of construction known in high-quality guitars where the neck and headstock are one long unit. Even though the guitar has one long neck, it also features several wood pieces glued to it. But that doesn't stop at the body, continuing through the tail of the guitar.

2. Material

The type of material used to construct a guitar is vital, but you shouldn't judge the guitar's durability solely on the type of material used for its construction. But consider a guitar that was made of better materials as they would last longer and stand the test of time.

Wood

Wood is the most common type of material used in constructing guitars. When manufacturers use expensive or rare wood to construct a guitar, it will affect the price. We can classify the quality of wood used in constructing guitar into three different criteria, namely:

- *Types*

The type of wood used is the first criterion we will be looking into. Different types of wood used include mahogany, maple, and rosewood, amongst others. Rosewood is the most preferred choice of hardwood used in constructing guitars, but they tend to be the most expensive wood followed by maple, then mahogany.

- *Style*

We can also classify the type of wood used in constructing the guitar by looking at the wood's region and grain styles. Brazilian rosewood is redder and grainier than East Indian rosewood, but they are more expensive. Figured maples like the flame and quilted are more expensive than bird's-eye or rock maples.

- *Grade*

Lastly, guitar manufacturers use a grading system from A to AA (being the highest) to evaluate the wood based on grade, color, and consistency. High-grade wood is used for constructing a high-quality guitar.

3. Tuner and Bridge Assemblies

In most expensive instruments, you can easily upgrade components, including hardware. But in terms of guitar, there are only a few options you can upgrade, like the bridge assembly and tuner. You can upgrade your tuner from the cheaper chrome-plated tuners to something more luster like gold-plated or black-matte. Similarly, you can upgrade the bridge assembly, knobs, and switches amongst other areas as well.

4. Workmanship

When buying expensive guitars, the workmanship that went into place in the construction needs to be more than perfectly fine. You can inspect the acoustic guitars interior just to make sure there are no fussy constructions done inside. Acoustic guitars less than the $600 range is only logical to find a few gapless joints. In essence, playing an expensive guitar should be a smooth ride.

Stringing a Guitar

When it comes to stringing a guitar, you either choose the steel strings or nylon strings. Below are steps you can use to change the strings as well as tune it.

Stringing Steel-String Guitar

Stringing a steel-string on an acoustic guitar can be a tricky thing to do. To change or restring your guitar involves two main steps. The first step is attaching the string to your bridge. Next, you need to attach the strings to the tuner which you can use to tighten the string's tension.

Step 1: Attaching the String to the Bridge

1. Use a needle-nose plier to pry up the bridge pin.

2. Place the end of the new string (called the ball or string ring) inside the role where you removed the bridge pin

3. Wedge the bridge pin firmly. Place the bridge pin such that the bridge slot faces forward toward the nut.

4. Gently pull the string until the ball rests against the bottom of the bridge pin

5. Test the string by gently tugging on it

Step 2: Securing the String to the Tuners

1. Pass the string through the hole in the post

2. Kink the metal wire towards the guitar

3. Rotate the peg clockwise to tighten the string to the post

Stringing Nylon-String Guitar

Another common type of string that is quite different from stringing a steel-string acoustic guitar is the nylon-string. Nylon strings guitar does not use bridge pins; rather, the strings are tied off. Similarly, the headstock of nylon strings guitars is slotted and has rollers as opposed to posts.

Step 1: Attaching the String to the Bridge

1. To remove the old string, loosen the string from the slotted rollers, and then remove it from the bridge.

2. Pass one end of the new string through the hole of the bridge and leave about 1 ½ inch sticking out the rear of the hole

3. Secure the string by bringing the short end over the bridge and passing it under the long part of the string. Then pass the short end under, over, and then under itself, on the top of the bridge.

4. With one hand, pull the long end of the string while moving the knot with your other hand such that excess slack is removed, causing the knot to lie flat on the bridge.

Step 2: Securing the String to the Tuners

1. Pass the string through the hole in the tuning post. Bring the end of the string back and over the roller towards you and then pass under itself and in front of the hole.

2. Pass the short end under and over itself, creating a couple of wraps.

3. Wind the peg, so the strings wrap the loop you just formed, forcing it down against the post.

Turn the peg with the one hand to taut the string.

Chapter 4

Tuning the Guitar

After fixing all the strings on your guitar, you must tune the strings. Tuning the strings is a process of increasing or reducing the tension to produce a certain note. There are several ways you can tune a guitar. And in this chapter, we will be talking about the several ways you can tune the guitar. Your job is to decide which of the methods feels more comfortable for you. Because obviously, each method comes with its fair share of pros and cons. Your ears and your eyes are the most important part of tuning a guitar, so be sure to be very observant of any little change in pitch.

Tuning Your Acoustic Guitar Using the Basic Tuning Method

Another method of tuning the guitar is using relative tuning. It is so named because you do not need to use any outside reference to tune the guitar. While this method is one of the most versatile, it is not recommended that a beginner should use. To be able to use this method effectively, you need to know the sound of each string. And as a beginner who has little to no experience with the sound of each string, you'd find it difficult to use this method. This method will come in handy when you need to tune your guitar on stage while playing for the crowd.

As long as you tune your guitar properly, you can use it to create harmonious and sonorous tones. You'd know the strings of a guitar are in tune when the sound they produce is in a way related to one another. To tune the guitar using this method, you need to choose a starting point, say the 1st string. If possible, tune that string to pitch, then use that same string to start tuning all the other strings relative to the 1st string, which you started with. Similarly, you can use the 5th fret method to check if two strings are in tune. Because each string is related to each other, the sound of an opened string and the string above it on the 5th fret should resemble each other. As we proceed in this method, you'd get to understand better. Below are steps to use to tune your guitar using the basic tuning method:

1. Know the Name of Each String

First, you need to be able to identify each string and their names. As we said in previous chapters, there are six strings on an acoustic guitar. The strings are named E, A, D, G, B, and E in order of their thickness. The fattest string is the 1st string, which is the one closest to the ceiling when you hold the guitar in a playing position. The 1st string is called the low E string. The 2nd string is next to the 1st string, and it is called the A string. Similarly, the 3rd string is called the D string, 4th string the G string, 5th string the B string. And lastly, the thinnest string, which is closest to the floor when you hold the guitar in a playing position, is called the high E string.

2. Identify the Tuning Pegs for Each String

The next thing you need to do is find a way to identify the peg for each string. To achieve this, follow the string from the neck to the corresponding peg to make sure you are turning the right peg for the string. Before you start tuning, pluck the string a few times and turn the peg clockwise and anticlockwise, you'd hear the pitch of the string go up and down.

3. *Pluck Each String to Match the Correct Pitch*

This is the point of tuning a guitar using the most difficult method. Your ears need to be well trained to know when the string hits the right note. Pluck the string and adjust the peg. If the string's pitch is higher than the pitch of the note, the string should play, turn the peg such that it loosens the tension of the string. Similarly, if it is too low, turn the peg to taut the string. Repeat this step for all six strings on the guitar until you are satisfied with the sound of each string.

4. *Use the 5th-Fret to Match the Sound of the Strings Immediately Below*

To check if each of the strings is well-tuned, we are going to be using the 5th-fret method. On the 5th fret, the immediate string below it sounds the same when you play it open. The only exception is the B string, which must be held on the G string's 4th fret to tune it. In other words, when you pluck the low E or 1st string along with the immediate string below it i.e., the B string on the 5th fret, they should sound similar. Similarly, when you pluck the B string and hold the G string on the 4th fret, they should sound similar. Do this for all the strings and adjust as you see fit.

5. *Strum a Few Notes*

Finally, strum a few notes to check the intervals. You can play the C chord or any other first position chord to make sure the guitar is well-tuned.

Tuning Your Acoustic Guitar Using a Chromatic Tuner

Another all too common method you can use to tune the guitar is with a chromatic tuner. Using the chromatic tuner, it tunes your guitar more accurately than when you use your ears. Moreover, this is the recommended method for beginners and intermediate players who haven't trained their ears to detect the sound of each string. The only downside is that you have to spend extra to buy the chromatic tuner to use this method, and it only comes in handy when you have it on you when you need to tune your guitar.

Apart from the accuracy in your tuning this method offers, they can also quickly tune your guitar. Newer models of these tuners, especially the ones for guitar, can tell the string you are playing, as well as the current pitch of that string. If the string is too sharp (too high) or flat (too low), it would be indicated on the chromatic tuner. Follow the steps below to use this step to tune your guitar:

1. *Turn On the Chromatic Tuner*

The first thing you should do when using this method is to turn on the chromatic tuner. You need to place the tuner close to your guitar so that when you pluck the string, it will be able to pick the right pitch. You can set the tuner on a table and place the table close to the sound box. Also, ensure you set the chromatic tuner to measure the right instrument. The chromatic tuner isn't meant for tuning only a guitar. Some tuners are so versatile you can use it to tune guitar, piano, violin, and even woodwind instruments. So, set the tuner to tune acoustic guitar and not bass or electric guitar.

2. Pluck a String

Starting from the 1st string, pluck it firmly. As the string sounds, the chromatic tuner will read the pitch of the sounding string. On the digital screen, the name of the string you pluck will be displayed together with information whether the string is too flat or too sharp. Depending on the type of chromatic tuner you are using, but most tuners come with a graph-like screen. As such, you get the flexibility to tune your guitar in real-time.

3. Tune the String Down or Up

When you pluck the string and reads too flat on the tuner, you need to increase the string's tension. Keep plucking the string as the chromatic tuner keeps reading the pitch as you tighten the string. Keep tightening the string until you get to the middle between the flat area and the sharp area. Similarly, if it reads too sharp, it means the string is too tight, so you have to loosen it. Do the same thing for all the strings on the guitar.

4. Strum a Few Chords

Play a few chords on the guitar to make sure your guitar is well-tuned. You can strum the C chord or any other first position chord because they are easy and sound familiar.

Tuning Your Acoustic Guitar Using an Alternative Method

Apart from using your ears and a chromatic tuner, or electric tuner, there are other ways you can tune a guitar. We call these other ways of tuning a guitar the alternative method. The alternative method of tuning a guitar is to tune it to a fixed source; usually, another instrument, say a piano or a pitch pipe, for example. This method of tuning is perfect when you want to play the guitar with another instrument. In other words, the guitar will be in sync with this other instrument. The following describes how to tune the guitar using a fixed reference.

- *Using a Piano*

The piano is one of the most common instruments used to tune several instruments. People use the piano as a fixed source to tune other instruments because it holds pitch so well. Most often, a piano is tuned annually or biannually, depending on the conditions. Assuming you have a well-tuned piano around, or better still, an electronic keyboard, all you need to do is to match the open string to the appropriate keys on the piano. So, when you pluck the open low E string on the guitar, play the low E on the keyboard. Then tighten or loosen the tuners until the low E string is in tune. Play the next string on the guitar and make sure it is tuned. Repeat this process until all the strings on the guitar are well-tuned.

- *Using a Pitch Pipe*

You can easily tune your guitar without using a piano or an electric keyboard, using a pitch pipe. The pitch pipe can serve as a standard tuning reference when you need one. As a guitarist, you can use a special pitch pipe that plays only the notes of the open string of a guitar. One of the major advantages you have when using a pitch pipe to tune a guitar is the ability to hold it firmly in your mouth while blowing, freeing up your hands to tune the guitar properly. However, the disadvantage of using it is that sometimes it takes a while to get used to relating a wind-produced pitch against a struck-string pitch. In other words, it won't be easy for beginners to tune a guitar with a pitch pipe because it is a wind instrument, and a guitar is a string instrument.

Chapter 5

Developing Basic Playing Strategies

I n this chapter, we will be taking things a notch higher by going through some of the basics of playing the guitar. Being able to play the guitar goes beyond knowing the best guitar to pick out, or knowing how to string and tune it. Things like how to hold the guitar, how to manipulate your left and right fingers to make something melodious amongst others are what makes you a great guitarist. In this chapter, we will be going through the basic skills you need to possess. We will also be talking about some basic music-deciphering skills to give you a better chance to play your first chord.

Posture: Standing or Sitting with the Guitar

One of the first things you need to get comfortable with before we even proceed into the playing procedure is your posture. When playing a musical instrument, your posture has a significant impact on how well you play. With the guitar, you have the flexibility to choose between a sitting and a standing position. Whatever position you decide to choose will not affect the sound you make, but it will affect how comfortable you can play. We cannot stress it enough that you need to take a position that feels the most comfortable for you to get the best sound possible. You don't want a scenario where you are struggling with your posture and, at the same time, with navigating between chords and strumming patterns.

A lot of people prefer to sit when practicing as it gives them the tranquility to understand faster. But when performing in public, many people love to stand to give the crowd a kind of energy and vibe. The one exception that doesn't give you the option to stand or sit is with the classical guitar, which normally requires you to play in a seated position. This doesn't mean you can't play classical music while standing, but a more serious pursuit of classical-style guitar playing requires you to sit while playing. Don't let a faulty playing position limit your potential. Below are important tips to note about standing or sitting while playing the guitar.

- *Sitting Position*

Practicing how to play the guitar in a seated position lets you optimize your practice session by letting you practice more efficiently and precisely. Also, in a seated position, you get to overcome challenges like restriction in the range of hand movement, sloppy playing, and tension of your hand. Sitting while playing the guitar also gives you better accuracy and stamina, even while playing at high speed/tempo. Assuming you are right-handed, the correct way to hold the guitar will require you to rest the guitar's waist on your right leg.

Furthermore, ensure your feet are slightly apart to give the guitar a good balance by resting your right arm lightly on the bass bout. Do not support the guitar's neck with your left hand; it only restricts your hand from moving freely. You should also balance the guitar so that you can take your left hand completely off the fretboard without the guitar falling. Your back should be kept straight as you sit on the chair and shoulders relaxed. Avoid leaning back into the chair, even if you can still keep a straight back. Lastly, you can sit in front of a mirror so you can monitor your posture.

- ***Standing Position***

You can also play the guitar in a standing position. To play the guitar in this position, you need to strap the guitar to your shoulder to give you balance. When you fasten the strap to the pin on the guitar, you can then stand upright to avoid any tension while playing, giving your arms freedom so you can play many octaves with precision. While playing the guitar strapped to your shoulder is cool and gives you a Rockstar feeling, you must adjust the strap securely to comfortable playing height.

Playing the guitar with the strap being too high or too low will severely limit your playing ability. So, adjust the guitar such that it should be hanging high enough to give your hand the flexibility to move around. When you strap the guitar around your shoulder, the neck should be included upward at a 30 degrees angle. If you like, you can strap the guitar lower, but if you do, place your left leg on a box during a passage to allow you to extend your playing hand to access more octaves with ease.

Positioning the Hands

Perhaps you might already know this, but your left hand is your fretting hand, while your right hand is your strumming hand while playing the guitar. It takes skills to manipulate your fingers efficiently to form chords and move from one string to another smoothly and precisely. You also need to be music-oriented to understand the strumming patterns that suit what you are playing. Below are some tips to get you on the right path to properly positioning your hands.

- ***The Left-Hand Position***

The left hand, as we said earlier on, is the fretting hand, or fingering hand. To get an idea of the correct way your left hand should hold the guitar, stretch out your left hand, loose fist, and palm up, place your thumb roughly between your second and first fingers. Note, all of your knuckles should be bent. Your hand should look like that when you hold the guitar neck. Your thumb glides to the back of the guitar's neck, just like when you are making a fist but not as rigid. Your finger knuckles should stay bent, whether you are relaxed or fretting.

Left-hand fretting requires strength. So, don't be tempted to ignore the strength when you try to speed up; it will only affect your sound. Building up the strength of your left-hand takes a lot of time. Note, taking shortcuts mostly never works or may only worsen the case in the long run. The best way to build your left-hand strength is by playing the guitar consistently. The main thing to remember is keeping a good left-hand position that keeps you playing naturally and comfortably. Remember to stop and rest for a while when your hand starts to ache or hurt. As with any other activity involving muscle development, resting for a period to enable the body to catch up is important.

- ### *The Right-Hand Position*

On the other hand, the right hand is where the actual rhythm is produced on the guitar with strums. The best position to have your guitar while strumming it, either in a sitting or standing position, is at a 60 degrees angle to the strings. This position gives you an advantage when playing with a pick. But on the other hand, if you were using the fingerstyle playing, then you may want to turn your right hand more perpendicular to the string, bringing it as close to 90 degrees angle as possible. When playing an acoustic guitar, you can use either strum with a pick or your fingers.

Using a Pick

Whether you are playing pop, jazz, blues, rock 'n' roll, or country, using a pick produces a strong sound. Using a pick is often recommended when playing songs that involve strumming or striking mainly chords. The pick is held between the index finger and thumb, and the tip of the pick sticks out perpendicular to the thumb. When striking the string, your middle finger, ring finger, and pinky finger rests on the pickguard. You strike the string with the pick by using your elbow and wrist motion. The more vigorous you need to strum, the more elbow you must put into the mix. Try not to grip the pick too tightly while playing. Note, picks come in different gauges (gauge indicates how stiff or thick the pick is). Thinner picks are easier for beginners than heavy-gauge picks, which are mainly used by professionals.

Using Your fingers

You can also play the guitar with your right-hand fingers, especially when you fingerpick strings and not strum the strings. While fingerpicking, the thumb plays the bass or low E string. Also, when you are fingerpicking, play the strings with the tip of your fingers. Position your hand over the sound hole and keep the wrist stationary, but not rigid. Furthermore, maintaining a slight arch in your wrist so that your finger comes down more vertically on the string also helps. For example, when playing classical guitar, you must hold your fingers almost perpendicular to each other to enable you to draw against the string with enough strength.

Understanding Guitar Notation

Unlike other instruments, you don't need to read music to be able to play the guitar. Musicians have devised an easier and simpler way to communicate basic ideas like song structure, chord progression, chord construction, and rhythmic figures. Understanding this shorthand device for tablature, rhythm slashes, and chord diagram sets you on the fast lane to playing the guitar in no time.

A Chord Diagram

Reading a chord diagram for a guitar is different from that of music; it's far simpler. All you need to do is understand the frets, strings, and where to put your fingers to form the chord. A chord is a simultaneous sounding of three or more notes. Below is an anatomy of a chord chart, and following after it is a briefing of what the different parts of the diagram mean:

- The grid with vertical lines and horizontal ones represents the guitar fretboard. It is more or less the guitar's view, as if you stand on a chair and place the guitar on the floor.

- The horizontal lines represent the frets. The thick line at the top of the grid is the guitar's nut, where the fretboard ends. Meaning, the 1st fret is the second vertical line from the top.

- The vertical lines represent the strings of the guitar. The vertical line at the far right is the high E or 1st string, while the vertical line at the far left is the low E or 6th string.

- The dots on the grid represent the notes that you fret.

- On the dots, there are numbers assigned to each dot. The number indicates the finger you are to use to fret that note. Since you can only fret the guitar with four fingers, the index finger is represented by 1, the middle finger by 2, the ring finger by 3, and the little/pinky finger by 4.

- Lastly, the O and X symbol above some strings indicates the strings that you should leave open or not play. The O symbol indicates an open string, while the X symbol indicates a string you don't pick or strike.

Rhythm Slashes

Rhythm slashes are slash marks musicians use to indicate how to play a rhyme but not what to play. So, after determining a chord to play, the slash mark tells you how to play it. For example, see the picture below.

For example, the G chord with four slashes beneath it shows you that you are to finger the G chord and strike it four times. Following that is the D and A chords, beneath it are four slashes. You are to strike the D chord twice, then change to the A chord and strike that twice as well. With the rhythmic slashes, you can easily know when you need to change chords and how many times you are to strike the strings.

Tablature

Lastly, let's take a look at tablature. Tablature is a notation system that is used to represent the strings and frets of the guitar graphically. While a chord diagram shows you what finger to use and where the finger should go, tablature shows you how you play music over some time. The picture below shows two staff, a tablature, and a standard music notation staff. The second staff shows exactly what is going on in the regular musical staff above it. Tablature, sometimes called the guitar tab, does not show you what notes to play as in Eb or F# or C, but it, however, tells you what string to fret and where exactly on the fretboard to fret that string.

The picture below shows us some examples of sample notes and where to play them on the guitar. From the treble clef, you can see that the first note to play is the low E, which on the guitar tab reads 0. The 0, in that case, indicates the 6th string or low E being played opened. Next is the F note on the tablature, which is being played on the second fret with the index finger held with the 6th string. The G note on the tablature is played with the ring finger on the third fret of the 6th string. The same procedure is applied to all the notes on the tablature.

How to Play a Chord

After understanding what the guitar notation describes in the preceding section, your best bet is to jump in and play your first chord. Chords are the building blocks of songs. By strumming chords, you can make a song with the guitar. You can't just smack any group of notes; you must play a group of notes organized in some meaningful arrangement. To begin, you can start with a fairly simple chord like the C chord because it is particularly guitar-friendly. When you get the hang of playing a chord, you will find out that you can move several of your fingers into position simultaneously. It is alright to place your fingers one at a time on the frets and strings for now. Use the instruction below to hold a C chord properly:

1. Place your index finger on the 2nd string, 1st fret, and press it down hard. Apply enough pressure to keep your finger from moving off the string. The key to holding a string properly is to hold it a bit closer to the fret.

2. Press the 4th string with your middle finger at the 2nd fret. At this stage, your first and middle fingers should be on the 2nd and 4th strings with an unfretted string on the 3rd string.

3. Lastly, place your ring finger on the 5th string, 3rd fret, and press it down firmly. You may need to spread your hand out a bit, and your thumb is grasping the back of the neck properly.

Strum the strings to play the C chord. When holding the guitar strings, ensure you use your fingertip to press down the string. Don't relax your finger but make sure they stand upright on the strings. You can pick an individual string to check if you are holding all the strings right. If you hear a buzzing sound, that means you are either not holding the string properly, or one of your fingers is interfering or resting on the string. You can fix the buzz by adjusting that finger without removing your fingers from the string, then strum the chord again, and make sure you get it right.

Chapter 6

The Fretboard

F rom the preceding chapter, you must have learned one or two things about the fretboard. Understanding the fretboard is quite important to understanding chords and progressions on the guitar. As a beginner, learning a couple of notes on the fretboard is quite important. But learning all the possible notes that can be formed on the fretboard is another ball game entirely. Learning all the notes on the fretboard is an arduous task, but it is worth it in the long run. Knowing the fundamentals of the guitar makes the learning process a lot easier to tackle.

Naming the Notes on the Fretboard

On the guitar and in the western music generally, we have seven notes ranging from A to G. These notes can be sharp or flat depending on how you are counting the notes. If you are going up the scale, you often count the notes as sharp. It is always seen as a flat if you are going down the scale. In some cases, a single note can be referred to as a flat or sharp at the same time. For example, C#/Db, which reads C sharp, or a D flat. You can play either of the notes, and you will get the same sound.

Guitar playing is more interesting when you have a firm understanding of the notes of the fretboard. A standard classical acoustic guitar has 19 frets, but the frets can go as high as 21 or even 24 frets on some models. But for the sake of this section, we will be explaining how the notes on the first 12 frets are formed to give you all you need to advance your playing skills. Below is a picture that summarizes it all, and after the picture, you'd understand the reason behind each note naming.

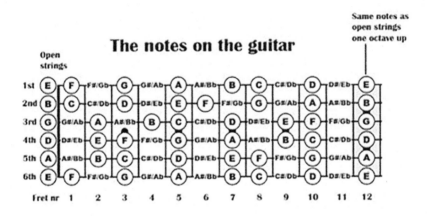

From the picture above, you may wonder why the octave is on the 12th fret. One would expect that the octave should be on the 8th fret, so why the 12th? On the guitar, the octave is not just the notes spread out over eight notes, but eight naturals. That means you are not going to be counting the flats and sharp when counting the octave. Take the 1st string; for example, the first note is the E, followed by F, G, A, B, C, D, and E, which makes a total of eight notes of an octave different. In other words, on the guitar, it takes 12 frets to get you an octave higher than a particular note.

• *1st String*

The 1st string is the thinnest string on the guitar, as you already know. And the 1st string is the E string, as you should also already know. When you play the 1st string without holding anything on the fret, you'll produce an E note sound. Things get a little different when you depress the 1st string on the first fret; you'll get an F note sound. Normally, you should have expected to hear an E# or Fb sound, but these notes do not exist, at least not on the guitar.

Moving to the next fret, depressing and striking the 1st string on the second fret will produce an F# or Gb note. In this case, we get an accidental note, which we didn't get in the first fret. This is because the F#/Gb note exists. The third fret is the G note; you guessed it right. And the fourth fret is an A because there is no H note in music generally. As we said earlier, you move from A to G, then go back to A; repeat the same cycle over and over again. After the A on the fifth fret, we have an A# or Bb note on the sixth fret.

Now, take note, on the seventh fret, things get a little tricky again, as the note moved from B on the seventh fret to a C on the eighth fret. This is because there can't be a B# or a Cb note. After the C note on the seventh fret, the next note on the ninth fret is the C# or Db note. On the tenth fret, we have the D note and, on the eleventh fret, the D# or Eb note. Lastly, we have the E note on the twelfth fret. The E registered on the twelfth fret is an octave higher than the open high E string.

- *2nd String*

The 2nd string is the next thinnest string or the B string, as you already know. When you play the 2nd string without holding anything on the fret, you will get a sounding B note, hence the name the B string. Based on our explanation, when you move from the first fret on the B string to the second fret, you shouldn't expect to hear a B# or Cb note, but a sounding C. As we explained earlier, the B# or Cb notes do not exist on the guitar. It can be a bit confusing because of the nature of the guitar's fret, which is a half-step apart, you would expect to encounter an accidental after every natural note, but in the case of the B to C, there are none.

When we move to the third fret, depressing and striking it should produce a D note. Similarly, when we move from the third fret to the fourth fret, you will get a D# or Eb note. And on the fifth fret, you will get the E note. Things get a bit different again when we move from the fifth fret to the sixth fret on the 2nd string, as there are also no accidentals between the E note and F note.

Moving from the sixth fret to the seventh fret, you'd get a sounding F# or Gb note. And as you can already guess, the note after the flat is the natural; on the eighth fret, you'd get a G note. On the ninth fret, we have the G# or Ab note. Likewise, on the eleventh fret, we have the A# or Bb note, which brings us to the last fret the twelfth fret. On the twelfth fret, we have the B note, which is an octave higher than the open B string.

- *3rd String*

The 3rd string is also known as the G string, and it is located just above the 2nd string. The technique we used in counting the notes on the 1st, and 2nd string also applies to this string. In other words, the notes still vary from A to G, and there are no accidentals between B and C, as well as E and F. So when you play the G string opened without pressing anything on the fret, you should hear a G note, hence the name of the string. But when you press the 3rd string on the first fret, you should hear a G# or Ab note.

With that being established about the 3rd string, the second fret is where the A note begins, not the first fret as you may have presumed because after G is A. But next time, try not to forget about the accidentals. Moving from the second fret to the third fret, we have an A# or Bb note. On the fourth fret, we have the B note. But moving from the fourth fret to the fifth fret, there are no accidentals. In other words, on the fifth fret, we have a C note and not a B# or Cb note.

Furthermore, on the sixth fret, we have C# or Db note. And as you would guess, the note after the sixth fret with the flat, the D note, is the note on the seventh note. The D# or Eb note is the note on the eighth fret. And on the ninth fret, we have the E note. And as you would have it, between the ninth fret and tenth fret, there are no accidentals between you are moving from E to F note. On the eleventh fret, we have the F# or Gb note. And lastly, on the twelfth fret, we have the G note, which is an octave higher than the open G string.

- *4th String*

The 4th string is also known as the D string, as you already know, and it is a pretty thick string. It is located between the G string and the A string. When you play the 4th string without pressing any fret, it will produce a D note sound, hence the string's name. But when you on the first fret of the D string is a D# or Eb note. Similarly, on the second fret of the 4th string is the flat's natural note on the first string.

To move from the second fret to the third fret, use the same technique we have been using to name and count notes from the 1st string so far. Moving from an E note will always be to an F note because there are no accidentals between these two notes on the guitar's fretboard. Moving forward, on the fourth fret, we have the F# or Eb note. Next to that, on the fifth fret, we have the G note. After the G note, we have the G# or Ab note on the sixth fret. On the seventh fret, we have the A note, and on the eight frets, we have the A# or Bb note.

On the ninth fret, we have the B note. But moving from the ninth fret to the tenth fret, there are no accidentals. As we explained earlier, moving from B will always be to a C note because there are no accidentals between these notes. So, on the tenth fret, we have the C note. Furthermore, on the eleventh fret, we have the C# or Db note. Lastly, we have the D note on the twelfth fret, which is an octave higher than the open D string.

- **5th String**

The 5th string is the second thickest string on the guitar, and it is also called the A string. When you play the 5th string without holding any fret, the sound produced is an A note, hence the name. But when you press the 5th string on the first fret, you will produce an A# or Bb note. And after that, the second fret produces a B note sound. And as we have been saying after the B note is supposed to be a B# or Cb note, but there is no such note on the guitar. So, moving from the second fret to the third fret is a C note.

After the note on the third fret is the C# or Db note on the fourth fret. On the fifth fret, we have the D note. If a fret has a flat, the next fret will be the flat's natural fret. If we have a D# or Eb note on the sixth fret, you should be able to guess the note of the next fret with ease. If you think the note on the seventh fret is the E note, then you are correct.

Following the same naming pattern, the note after the seventh fret is the F note on the eighth fret because there is no accidental between the E and F notes. On the ninth fret, we have the F# or Gb note, while on the tenth fret, we have the G note. On the eleventh fret, we have the G# or Ab note, which brings us to the last note on the twelfth fret, which is the A note. The A note is an octave higher than the open A string.

- **6th String**

Lastly, the 6th string, otherwise known as the low E string, is the thickest string on an acoustic guitar. Playing the 6th string open, without pressing any fret, will produce a low E note, hence the name. Since it is an E string, it will have the same naming pattern as the high E note, but we would still love to work you through the naming pattern, so you have a better understanding. After an E note, we always have an F note following after and not an accidental. So, on the first fret, we have the F note.

On the second fret, we have the F# or Gb note. Moving to the next fret, which is the third fret, we have the G note there. On the fifth fret, we have the G# or Ab note and on the sixth fret, we have the A note. Following that, we have the A# or Bb note on the sixth fret and on the seventh fret, we have the B string. Take note of the movement from the seventh to the eighth fret as there are no accidentals between B and C notes. So, on the eighth fret, we have the C note.

Similarly, on the ninth fret, we have the C# or Db note. After that, on the tenth fret, we have the D note. On the eleventh fret, we have the D# or Eb note. Lastly, on the twelfth fret, we have the low E note, which is an octave higher than the opened low E string.

To sum things up, when counting notes on the fret of a guitar, moving from B – C and E – F does not have any accidents, i.e., there can't be a flat or a sharp in-between them. With this in mind, you can master the notes of any fret with ease. We have named the first twelve notes on the fretboard of all acoustic guitars; you can follow this same naming technique to name the full notes on your guitar's fretboard. When you are done, you can compare it with materials you can find online.

Chapter 7

Understanding Music Notation

Knowing the names of strings on the fretboard is great, but that is not all you need to be a great guitarist. The guitar is a musical instrument, so having a basic understanding of the music notation is paramount. Although note reading music is not necessary when it comes to guitar playing, it is helpful to understand music notation. In this chapter, we will be talking about everything you need to understand the musical notation related to a guitarist. By the end of this chapter, you should be able to read music as quickly and easily as possible. So, familiarize yourself with the written symbols and notation practices used in this book so you can better understand the written exercises and pieces in this book.

Understanding Music Notation

When you think about the standard notation for a guitar, what comes to mind is the staff, clef, and notes, just like you would find on the piano, flute, violin, and saxophone. So, to begin, let us start with a little bit of symbol introduction. In the following section, we covered music notation even deeper, with three of the main elements of music: pitch, duration, and expression/articulation.

The Composer's Canvas: The Staff, Clef, Bar-Lines, and Measures

Over the century, the system of writing music keeps constantly changing with new and better approaches. When musicians write music today, they don't simply write it on just any old piece of paper. The blank canvas isn't totally blank. In other words, musicians write music on a series of horizontal grids that hold the notes and other musical symbols. Below is an example of a canvas composer written music:

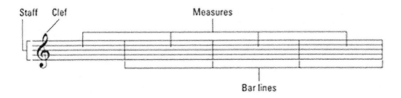

- ***Staff***

In general, musical staff refers to a grid of five lines and four spaces. The staff is used to indicate the different pitches in music. There are different staff types, but the bass and treble staff are the most common types. But in guitar playing, we will be looking mainly at the treble staff because most notes on the guitar are high pitched located on the treble staff. As we said earlier, there are five lines and four spaces on a staff, and each line and space are named according to the type of staff. On a treble staff, starting from the first line to the fifth line, the lines are named E, G, B, D, and F. And the four spaces on a treble staff from the first space is named F, A, C, and E. Notes at the bottom of a treble staff are low pitched, and the higher you go on a treble staff, the higher the pitch of the note.

- *Clef*

Just like we have staff, the clef is what determines what kind of staff we are dealing with. The clef is the first symbol you will see at the beginning of every staff. The two most common types of clef are the bass and treble clef. The guitar uses the treble clef as we said earlier, and we can also call it the G clef. The G clef resemblance to the letter G and the curlicue symbol wrapped around the G line of the staff or the second line from the bottom, which is the G line. These are the reasons for its name.

- ***Measures and Bar-Line***

Additionally, apart from the staff and clef we just explained, you must also have some sort of context in which to place notes in time. Most music has a beat or pulse that gives the music a particular rhythmic unit that the notes playoff. In turn, the beat is usually felt in larger groups of two, three, or even four. This division is represented on the staff with vertical lines that separate the music into sections called measures or bars. The section between two vertical lines is a measure, and the vertical lines themselves are called bar lines. Grouping music into measures makes it manageable by organizing the notes into a smaller unit that supports the beat's natural emphasis.

Pitch: The Low and High

As said earlier on, the pitch of a note indicates the highness or lowness of that note. So, when writing music notation, the notes are placed on different lines or spaces, indicating different pitches. Take your time to study the diagram below as it shows the breakdown of the various symbols and definitions that can be used to describe different pitches in musical notation. The diagram below is labeled number 1 through to 4, so we will be taking things numerically, giving their real names.

Pitch names: G A B C   G F♯ E D   A B C A   G♯ B♭ A♭ B

- *Note*

As we explained previously, notes are either placed on a line or in-between the line on a space. Wherever you place the note, a given staff tells us the pitch of that note. Notes placed closer to the bottom of the staff usually have a lower pitch than those placed higher up. In other words, from the diagram above, the first note on the diagram is a G note, while the next one is the A note. Since the G note is placed at a lower position than the A note, it is expected to have a lower pitch. The names of the five staff lines from the bottom to the top are E, G, B, D, and F. And the notes on the four spaces in between the lines spells the word face, as in F, A, C, and E.

- *Ledger Lines*

The note can fall above or below the staff as well as within the staff. In a case where the note falls outside the staff, they are written on ledger lines. Notes written on ledger lines tell you that the pitch falls higher or lower than the staff. When using ledger lines, think of it as a short or temporary staff line. The same rules apply as when you name notes on the lines and spaces within the staff. For example, let us consider the first ledger line below the staff, it is named, while the first ledger line above the staff is A. If you were to count the notes from the bottom F to the ledger line below it, or from the upper F note to the ledger line, you'd verify it yourself.

- *Accidentals*

Accidentals, otherwise known as flats, sharps, and naturals, are found in literally everything involving music. Accidentals are notes outside the key that are defined by their key signature. A sharp is used when you want to raise the pitch higher by a semitone. Similarly, a flat is used when you want to lower the pitch by a semitone. You use the natural accidental when you want to cancel the effect of the sharp or flat. Also, in some cases, an accidental can cancel a previous accidental or reinstate it.

- *Key Signature*

When you see a flat or a sharp beginning the staff immediately after the clef, it is called a key signature. A key signature tells you which notes to play as a sharp or as a flat for an entire piece, or at least the piece's major section unless otherwise stated. For example, from the diagram above, the key signature is sharp on the fifth line or F note, meaning every note placed on the fifth line, you will have to play it a half step higher. In other words, the key signature, in the case of the diagram, sends a loud and clear message all F's are sharp.

Duration: How Long to Hold a Note

Now that we understand the basics of music notation the staff, let's proceed a step further into durations. Durations are symbols used in staff to indicate the length of time a note should be played in a beat. Apart from using different pitches to create rhythm, the note's duration can also be used to create rhythm. The combination of pitch and rhythm makes music. Rest is also a type of duration indicating a musical silence. Also, note that by adding a tie to a note, you can increase the note's length, which connects one note to another of the same pitch. Below is a diagram of some of the common symbols used to indicate duration and symbols in a musical excerpt.

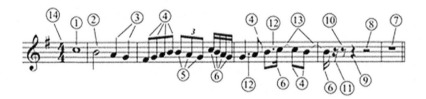

1. Whole Note

The whole note is a note having the time value of four beats in 4/4 time or four crotchets. The whole note is the longest note in use. Other notes you play on staff are fractions or multiples of a whole note.

2. Half Note

A half note, otherwise known as a minim, is a note played twice a quarter more and half the period of a whole note. In a note with a time signature, 4/4, the half note is two beats long.

3. *Quarter Note*

A quarter note is also known as crochet, is a note that is played one-quarter of the period of a whole note. Musicians often make the mistake of thinking a quarter note is one beat. But in reality, a quarter note is not always a beat, it may or may not be a beat depending on the context in which it's being used.

4. *Eight Note*

Eight note, also known as quaver, is a note you play for 1/8 the period you will play a whole note. It is possible to have a group of two or more eight notes on a scale beamed together. In such a case, split the note accordingly, but still within the eight note's time signature.

5. *Eight-Note Triplet*

An eight-note triplet is a group of three notes played in two eighth notes space of the same rhythmic value.

6. *16th Note*

A sixteenth note, also known as a semiquaver, is a note in a musical staff played for half the eight note duration. Similarly, two or more sixteenth notes can be beamed together.

7. *Whole Rest*

A whole rest is an interval of silence in the staff, which is equal to the period of one half of a breve rest or two half rest. In a 4/4-time signature, a whole rest is four beats.

8. Half Rest

Half rest with a symbol shaped like a small rectangle sits on a staff line indicating two beats' rest in a 4/4-time signature.

9. Quarter Rest

A quarter rest is a period of silence that is equal in length to a quarter note. A quarter rest can last for one beat in a 4/4-time signature. The quarter rest is a ¼ value of a whole beat. So, for the duration of one beat, no note will be played.

10. Eighth Rest

Eight rest with a symbol shaped like a middle-line note head extends upward instead of downward and used to denote a half beat's rest in 4/4.

11. 16th Rest

The 16th rest, with a symbol shaped like a two eight rest, it is used to indicate a quarter beat's rest in 4/4.

12. Augmentation

Augmentation is a symbol shaped like a dot that you see to the right of a rest or a note head, telling you when to rest or increase the note's length by half its original value. For example, a quarter note is one beat so a dotted quarter note will be 1 ½ beat.

13. Tie

The tie is a symbol of a curved line that joins two notes of the same pitch. You play the first note for its full value, and instead of restriking the second (tied) note, you let the note sustain for the combined value of both notes.

14. Time Signature

Lastly, the time signature is a two-digit symbol usually found at the beginning of a stay. With the time signature, you can count the beats in a measure and tell which beat to give emphasis or stress. For example, a 4/4-time signature means you are to play four beats to the measure, with the quarter note receiving the beat or pulse.

Expression and Articulation

You will see other symbols in a written piece apart from the basic elements like pitch and duration. Symbols used to represent expression and articulation give you a range of instructions, from navigating instruction to repeating a certain passage and playing the music expressively. Below is a diagram used to describe some of these symbols:

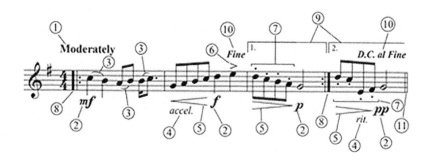

1. Tempo Heading

From the diagram, the symbol labeled 1 is the tempo heading, which is a word or phrase used to give guidance on the speed or feel of a piece. Sometimes the tempo heading is written in Italian such as Adagio, Andante, and Moderato. And sometimes, you may see the tempo heading written in the native language of the composer, like in the case of the diagram above, with the tempo heading "Moderately."

2. Dynamic Marking

The symbol labeled 2 in the diagram above represents the dynamic marking, which is a letter used to tell you how soft or loud you should play. Similarly, the dynamic marking is often an abbreviation of Italians words like mf for mezzo-forte, which means you should play medium loud. Other dynamic symbols include mp, p, f, ff, and pp.

3. Slur

The symbol labeled 3 in the diagram above is the slur, which is a curved line between two notes of different pitch. The slur tells you to connect the second note smoothly to the first note. You will often see a slur in a piece that requires a legato approach where the notes blend in an uninterrupted and sustained fashion.

4. Accelerando and Ritardando

The symbol labeled 4 in the diagram abbreviated as accel. It is an accelerando that tells you how fast you should play. In some cases, it may be written as ritard. Which means ritardando telling you how slow you should play.

5. *Crescendo and Decrescendo*

The symbol labeled 5 in the diagram is the crescendo abbreviated as cresc. This symbol looks like an open wedge called hairpins by some musician. Crescendo tells you how long you should play. To tell you how soft you should play, the decrescendo or decresc. is used.

6. *Accent*

The symbol labeled 6 in the diagram is the accent shaped like a small caret-like or wedge marking above or below a note, telling you to place emphasis on the note by striking it harder than you would normally do.

7. *Staccato Dot*

The symbol labeled 7 in the diagram represents a staccato dot, which is a small dot placed above or below the note head telling you to play the note short and detached.

8. *Repeat Signs*

The symbol labeled 8 in the diagram represents a repeat sign, which is a special bar-line type symbol, it is used to tell you to repeat the measures between the signs.

9. *Ending Brackets*

The symbol labeled 9 in the diagram is the ending brackets used to separate different endings in a repeated section. The ending brackets in the diagram above suggest that you should play the measure under the first ending bracket the first time. And on the repeat, you should play only the second ending and skip the first ending bracket.

10. D.C. al Fine

The symbol labeled 10 in the diagram above represents D.C. al fine, which reads Da capo, Italian for "from the top to the end." This symbol tells you to go back to the beginning and play until you see the words, To Coda.

11. Double Bar-Line

Lastly, the symbol labeled 11 in the diagram represents two bar lines closely spaced together, which indicates the end of a section or if the line is a combination of a thick and thin pair of the end of a piece.

Chapter 8

Basic Major, Minor, and 7th Chords

So far, so good we have made so much progress, and if you can keep up at this pace, you will see yourself advancing before you know it. In this chapter, we will be introducing you to some of the basic major, minor, and the 7th chords you ought to know as a beginner. Well, you can't learn all the chords at once, but you have to start somewhere. And we found out that some chords are relatively easier to master than others, and they are used in our everyday songs. In other words, with this beginner's chord, you can still follow up with your favorite songs, which is one of the best ways to learn guitar chords.

There are so many possible chords on the guitar that we can't begin to write on each of them. If we are to cover all the possible chords you can learn on the guitar, then this book's pages will be running into thousands – not to exaggerate, of course. In a nutshell, the next sections are a group of chords in a family; you need to know how to play as a beginner. They are fairly simple chords to learn, to kick start you on the right part.

The Basic Major and Minor Chords

1. The A Family Chord

To begin this section in this chapter, we will be looking at the family chords. Family chords should be the first chords every beginner should learn because they are relatively very easy to play. They contain a lot of open strings, which means you only have to press a few strings. Chords with open strings are called open position chords or open chords. The famous sound "Fire and Rain" by James Taylor is a perfect example of where the family chords were used. The basic chords in this family are the A, D, and E and each chord in the A family chord is known as a major chord. Take note, in guitar, notes names without any inscription beside it is always a major chord.

Fingering the A Family Chord

Since this is the first chord you will be held on the guitar, we will be walking you through how to go about it. And the first thing to note is to ensure you use the ball of your fingertip to press the strings properly. Also, ensure you press the string just behind the fret and note on the fret. Arch your ginger such that the fingertip of your fingers falls perpendicular to the neck. Also, ensure your left-hand fingernails are short, so they don't prevent you from pressing the strings down properly. Below you will find diagrams of the A family's basic chord – A, D, and E chords on the guitar.

Take note of the strings you press and play. Don't play strings marked with an X like the 6th string in the A chord and the 5th and

6th strings in the D chord. Selectively stringing the guitar may seem awkward at first, but it will feel quite natural after a few attempts.

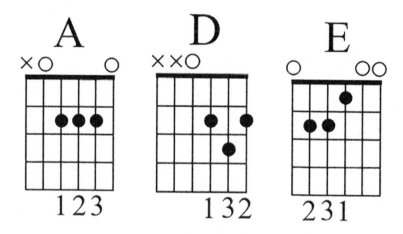

2. The D Family Chord

Another basic chord you should learn as a beginner is the D family chord. This chord consists of the D, Em, (read as E minor), G, and A chords. The D family chord shares two chords in the A family chord, the A and D chords, and introduces two new chords: the Em and G chords. Since you already know how to play the A and D chords from the preceding section, we will focus more on explaining how to play the new chords. The song, Here Comes the Sun by the famous musicians the Beatles is a popular song you will hear the use of D family chords.

Fingering the D Family Chord

The diagram below shows you how to hold the Em and G chords in the D family on the guitar. You may or may not have noticed, but none of the strings in the diagram below have an X symbol, which indicates you are to strike all the strings to get the chord's full sound. A trick you can use to hear the difference between the major and minor chord qualities is to play the E, the major chord described in the A family chords.

To play the E chord, simply press down the 3rd string on the first fret when you hold Em note. Strike the chord you are holding, then lift your finger on the 3rd string up and strike again to hear the sound quality difference when you move from a major to a minor. Another cool thing to note is the alternative fingering pattern for the G chord. You can hold the G chord either with the 1-2-3 or 2-3-4 fingers. As a beginner, you may want to stick to the 1-2-3 configuration, but as you advance and your fingers gain more strength and flexibility, you should switch to the 2-3-4 configuration instead. Why may you ask? Well, because it is easier and faster to switch to other chords when using the 2-3-4 fingering for G.

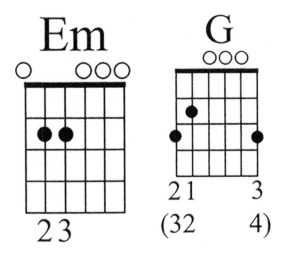

3. The G Family Chord

For those who would love to take things a notch higher, the G family chord is just right for you. The G family chord consists of G, Am, C, D, and Em chords. And as you carry over your knowledge from one family to another, you'll spot that we already looked at the D, Em, and G chords. As such, our focus in this chapter is on the A minor and C chords. If you are a bit confused about this family's sound, listen to the popular song "You've Got a Friend" by James Taylor to hear the sound of a song that uses the G family chords.

Fingering the G Family Chords

In the diagram below is the fingering pattern for playing the Am and the C chords. Note that these new chords played in the G family have similar finger patterns. Each chord has the index finger on the 2nd string of the first fret. Again, the middle finger is holding the 4th string on the second fret for both chords. In other words, keeping both the index finger and middle finger in place makes switching between the two chords easier.

Keep in mind switching chords is always easier when the chords have similar fingering patterns. When a chord shares similar notes, they are called common tones. Take note of the X over the 6th string in each of the chords below. Don't play the string while strumming either the Am or the C chords.

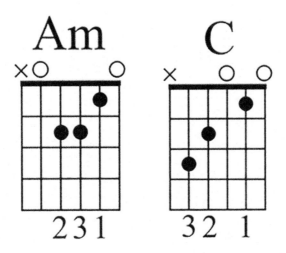

4. The C Family Chord

Lastly, we will be discussing the C family chords in this chapter. Although they are a bit more technical to wrap your hands around, they are one of the beginner's chords to learn. Some people even claim that C is the easiest key to play in. Moreover, the C is sort of the center point where everything literally begins in music. In actuality, there are too many chords in the C family to master. The basic chords that make up the C family are C, Dm, Em, F, G, and Am. But if you practiced the preceding section on the A, D, and G family chords, you should already know how to play the C, Em, and Am chords. So, in this section, we will be introducing you to the newer Dm and F chords. "Dust in the Wind" by Kansas makes use of the C family chords.

Fingering the C Family Chords

The diagram below shows that both the Dm and F chords have the second finger on the 3rd string and second fret. As such, holding the common string down makes switching between these two chords a breeze. Many people find the F chord particularly challenging and difficult to play of all the basic chords. This is because the F uses a barre. A barre is a scenario in chord formation when you use one finger to press down two or more strings at once. As in the F chord, the barre is at the 1st and 2nd string on the first fret.

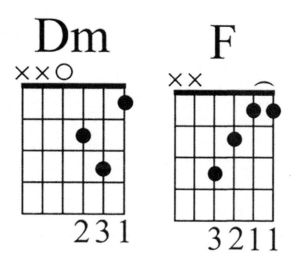

Basic 7th Chords

The basic 7th chords, otherwise known as the open position 7th chords, are easy to play like the simple minor or major chords. However, basic 7th chords produce a more complex sound than the basic minor and major chords. Players who have developed their basic major and minor skills will appreciate the basic 7th chords more. Moreover, you need to be well-trained before knowing where to substitute an ordinary major or minor chord for a 7th chord. The 7th chords make jazz music sound jazzy, and blue music bluesy.

There are different variants of the 7th chords with different sound and quality. This section will focus on three of the most common and important types you will encounter in playing the guitar: dominant 7th, minor 7th, and major 7th.

1. Dominant 7th Chords

The dominant 7th chord refers to the 5th degree of a major scale. If you are talking about the C7 or any 7 chords, you refer to the dominant 7th chord. Note that these notes are purposely called the dominant 7th merely to differentiate them from other types of 7th chord like the minor 7th and major 7th. Popular sounds that the dominant 7th chord was used to make are the likes of "I Saw Her Standing There" by the Beatles and "Wooly Bully" by Sam the Sham and the Pharaohs.

- **G7, D7, and C7**

The first group of dominant 7th chords we will be talking about are the G7, D7, and C7 chords. These chords are common open dominant 7th chords shown in the diagram below and how to finger them on the guitar. Note, if you already know how to play the C from the preceding section, you can form the C7 by adding your pinky finger on the 3rd string of the fourth fret. Also, take note of the Xs in the diagrams above the 5th and 6th string on the D7 chord; try not to play those strings when you strum. And at the same time, for the C7 chords, don't play the 6th string when you strum.

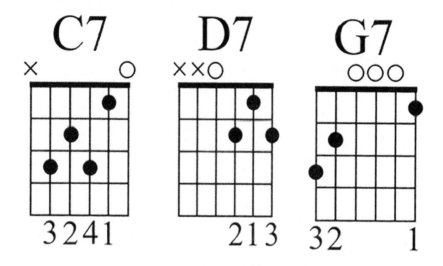

- ***E7 and A7***

Another two common chords that are often used to play songs from the dominant 7th chords are the E7 and A7 chords. The diagram below shows you how to play these chords. An easy way to play the E7 chord is from the E chord we explained earlier. By simply removing your third finger from the 4th string on the E chord, you can form the E7 chord. The version of E7 in this section shows you how to use only two fingers. You can also play an open position with four fingers, as we will describe it in the following section. But for now, acquaint yourself with this version of E7 until you can easily fret it quickly.

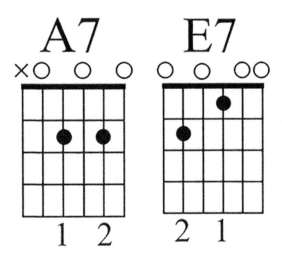

- ***E7 (Four-Finger Variant) and B7***

The last two popular chords we will be looking at in the dominant 7th chords are the E7 (four-finger variants) and the B7 chords. A lot of people think the four-finger version of the E7 is better sounding than the two-finger version. Playing this four-finger version of the E7 is quite easy, especially if you know how to play the E chord, simply add your pinky finger on the 2nd string of the third fret. In most songs, the B7 is often used along with the E7 to play certain songs. Don't forget to avoid striking the 6th string on the B7 chord.

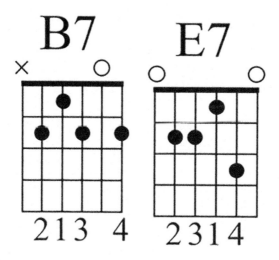

2. Minor 7th Chords: Dm7, Em7, and Am7

The minor 7th chords are quite different from the dominant 7th chords, in that their character is a little softer when played. The minor 7th chords are what you hear in the popular song "Light My Fire" by Doors. The diagram below shows you how to finger the three open positions of the minor 7th chords. Note that the Dm7 makes use of two string barres. In other words, you have to press down two strings with a single finger to play the Dm7 chord (in this case, the first finger is used to press the 1st and 2nd strings simultaneously at the first fret). The Dm7 note has common tones on the first and second fingers, with the F chord.

It helps you angle your finger slightly or rotate it on its side to fret those barre notes to play a barre chord. Ensure you hold those barre notes firmly to eliminate any buzzes in the sound you produce as you play the chord. The 5th and 6th strings on the Dm7 chord have Xs above them, so don't strike those strings as you strum. For the Am7, you finger the chord just like you will a C chord, only that you have to lift your third finger off to play the Am7.

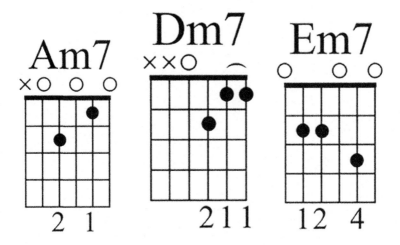

3. *Major 7th Chords: Cmaj7, Fmaj7, Amaj7, and Dmaj7*

Lastly, let's look at the major 7th chords you need to learn as a beginner. The major 7th chords sound brighter than the minor and dominant 7th chords. The popular song "Don't Let the Sun Catch You Crying" by Gerry and the Pacemakers is a common song you'd hear the use of the major 7th chords. The diagram below shows you how to finger the four open position major 7th chords on the guitar. Take note that the Dmaj7 has a three-string barre on the second fret with the index finger. Rotating your index finger to its side makes it easier to play the Dmaj7 chord. Also, don't play the 6th and 5th string marked X when strumming the Dmaj7 and Fmaj7 chords. And for the Amaj7 and Cmaj7, don't play the 6th string marked X while strumming.

When moving from the Cmaj7 to the Fmaj7 chord, take note that the middle finger and the ring finger move as a fixed shape across the strings in switching between these chords. Don't fret anything with your first finger when playing the Cmaj7 chord; rather, keep your first finger in a poised and curled position above the 2nd string on the first fret so you can bring it down quickly for the switch to Fmaj7.

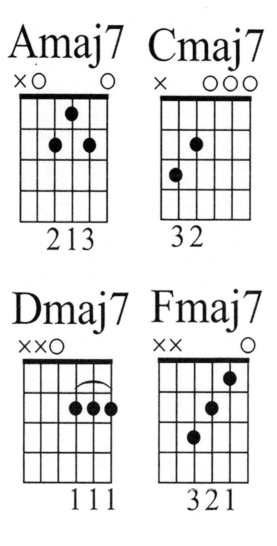

Chapter 9

Chord Technique

Chords, as you already know, are played with the left hand. And so far, so good; we have gone through a few of the basic chords you need to know as a beginner. So, in this chapter, we will take you further into the realms of how chords are formed on the guitar. Our major focus is on the Nashville number system. With a firm understanding of the Nashville number system, you will better understand why a chord is shaped the way they are.

This chapter will teach you how to form triad chords, 7th chords, 9th chords, 11th chords, and 13th chords, amongst others. In each of these chords, we will talk about their major, minor, diminished, and augmented, amongst others. There are more complex chord formations that may seem out of this world, but we will leave that for you to figure out as we believe by the end of this chapter, chord formation will become easy-peasy for you. But before we jump into the naming scheme, let's go through some basics you need to know before learning the Nashville number system.

Don't forget; you also have a role to play by learning more chords on your own as soon as you master these chords in this book. Remember, there are so many possible chords you can play on the guitar. So, learning a couple of new chords wouldn't hurt a fly. Also, for now, don't worry too much about what your right hand is supposed to do. We will figure that out in the next chapter, where we will discuss strumming patterns and everything your right hand should do.

Basics for Using the Nashville Number System in Chord Formation

As we already stated, the Nashville number system is a method used by musicians to transcribe music by denoting the scale degree on which a chord is built. With the Nashville number system, you can figure out chord progressions in no time. It is quite easy to wrap your head around. Rather than learning all the individual chords possible, you can use the Nashville number system to teach yourself new chords. The Nashville number system is so popular because of its flexibility, as it makes it easy to transpose songs and change the key of a sound without going through so much trouble. But before we go into the Nashville system's main details, let's take a look at these.

- ***Roots***

In every chord formation, there is always a root note. The root note often determines the name of the chord and the key of the chord. For example, when forming a major chord, and the root note is C, then the chord formation key will be the C major. Similarly, if it were a minor chord and the root note is A, then the chord formation key will be the A minor. In the Nashville number system, the first note in the chord is usually the root note.

- ***Body***

The body of a chord alters the function and sound of the chord. The body of a particular chord is affected by the type of chord you are playing, be it a major, minor, diminished, or augmented – they are all different.

- ***CAGED***

Another important thing you need to understand is the CAGED guitar system. The CAGED system maps out the fretboard into five sections by revealing the relationship between a note and common open chord shapes. CAGED is an acronym meaning the C chord, A chord, G chord, E chord, and D chord. Below is a diagram of how the CAGED system divides the fretboard.

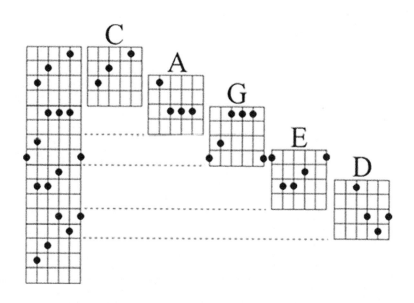

The Nashville Number System for Chord Formation

To use the Nashville number system, see the table below.

Key (1)	2	3	4	5	6	7
C	D	E	F	G	A	B
C#/Db	D#/Eb	F	F#/Gb	G#/Ab	A#/Bb	C
D	E	F#/Gb	G	A	B	C#/Db
D#/Eb	F	G	G#/Ab	A#/Bb	C	D
E	F#/Gb	G#/Ab	A	B	C#/Db	D#/Eb
F	G	A	A#/Bb	C	D	E
F#/Gb	G#/Ab	A#/Bb	B	C#/Db	D#/Eb	F
G	A	B	C	D	E	F#/Gb
G#/Ab	A#/Bb	C	C#/Db	D#/Eb	F	G
A	B	C#/Db	D	E	F#/Gb	G#/Ab
A#/Bb	C	D	D#/Eb	F	G	A
B	C#/Db	D#/Eb	E	F#/Gb	G#/Ab	A#/Bb

Major Chords

Major chords, as you already know, are the most common type of chords in music. As we said in the preceding chapters, major chords are written as a single letter. But in some cases, musicians use uppercase "M" to represent major chords. Since our interest is in chord formation, let's take a look at how to form triads, 7th, 9th, and 13 major chords using the Nashville numbering system.

- *Major Triad Chords*

A triad chord is a type of chord made up of three notes. They are the most common type of chord beginners learn. To construct a major triad chord, you need a root chord. Let us take C as the root chord in this case. If C is the root chord, then the following applies:

C- D – E – F – G – A

1 – 2 – 3 – 4 – 5 – 6

After numbering the scale, you need to apply the formula. The formula to use to form triad chords:

1 – 3 – 5

With this formula, you can construct any major triad chord provided you know the scale. For example, let's take a closer look at the C major chord. Using the formula and the C major scale from the table above, we can deduce that the C major triad chord will use C, E, and G notes. So, as long as the strings on the guitar have the configuration C, E, and G, it is a C major chord. Below is a diagram of a C major chords. You can check other fingering patterns for the C chord; the idea is that they will all have the same notes – C, E, and G.

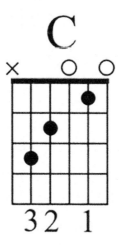

You can try the same example for other chords like the G chord. From the table at the end of this chapter and the formula for constructing triad chords, you can deduce that all G major chords should have notes G, B, and D. You can check with all the G major notes you know. The same principle applies to all the triad chords in the major scale.

- *Major 7th Chords*

To construct the major 7th chords, you need four notes. To construct a major 7th chord, let's take D as the root note in this case. If D is the root note, then the following applies:

$$D – E – F\#/Gb – G – A – B – C\#/Db – D$$

$$1 – 2 – 3 – 4 – 5 – 6 – 7 – 8$$

From the number above, all you need to do is apply the formula for writing a major 7th chord and get the note needed to draw a D major 7th chord. The formula for constructing major 7th chords is:

$$1 - 3 - 5 - 7$$

With this formula, you can construct any note in the major 7th chord. From the analogy above, applying the 1, 3, 5, and 7 gives you notes D, F#/Gb, A, and C#/Db to draw a Dmaj7 chord. Below is a diagram showing you the D chord's configuration using the same D, F#/Gb, A, and C#/Db notes. Likewise, you can check for other configurations of the D7 chord; you will notice it has the same fingering notes D, F#/Gb, A, and C#/Db.

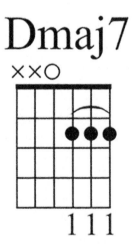

Similarly, you can try out the major 7th chords like the F. The F major 7th will have the notes configuration F, A, C, and E. If we are to take another example, say G, G major 7th will have the notes configuration G, B, D, and F#/Gb. The idea is to follow the formula 1, 3, 5, and 7, and remember always to use the natural 7th note.

- ***Major 9th Chords***

When we get to constructing major 9th chords, things get a bit more complex. Normally, after determining the root note and writing out that note's scale, we stop at a 7. For example, if we are to construct the C major 9th chords, that means C is the root note, then the following applies:

$$C - D - E - F - G - A - B - C - D - E$$

$$1 - 2 - 3 - 4 - 5 - 6 - 7 - 8 - 9 - 10$$

From the analogy above, you can see that after the 7th note, we didn't start again from 1, but an 8. In other words, 8 is also the same as 1, 9, is the same as 2, 10 is the same as 3, and so on. The formula for constructing major 9th chords is:

$$1 - 3 - 5 - 7 - 9$$

With this formula, you can construct any major 9th chord. Since we are considering the C chord, in this case, the C major 9th chords will have the notes C, E, G, B, and D. The diagram below shows the fingering of the Cmaj9 chord; you can confirm the notes in the chord to see it correlate to the notes we just deduced.

Cmaj9

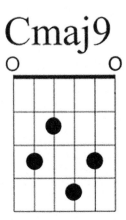

There are other configurations of the Cmaj9 apart from the diagram above; you can check it out. Let's also take a look at the Fmaj9 as another example. Using the formula, the Fmaj9 chord will have the following notes, F, A, C, and E. You can try out other major 9th chords and compare the notes to the fingering pattern.

- *Major 11th Chords*

Another type of major chords you'd come across as you learn is the major 11th chords. These chords are more complex, but you should learn them to help improve your playing skills. Like forming any chord, you need a root note. Once that is determined, write out the scale and apply the formula. As an example, let's construct the C major 11th chord. Since C is the root chord, the following applies:

$$C - D - E - F - G - A - B - C - D - E - F - G$$

$$1 - 2 - 3 - 4 - 5 - 6 - 7 - 8 - 9 - 10 - 11 - 12$$

From the above analogy, you can see that from the number 8 above is like another octave of the C scale. So, we can also read the 8 as a 1, 9 as a 2, 10 as a 3, and the list goes on and on. With that and the formula for constructing a major 11th chord, we can write the C major 11th chord. The formula for writing a C major 11th chord is as follows:

$$1 - 3 - 5 - 7 - 9 - 11$$

With this formula and the analogy given above, we can deduce that the notes for a major 11th chord must have C, E, G, B, D, and F. Below is a diagram of a C major 11th chord. You can check out for other examples of a C major 11th chord and compare the notes in the chord with the notes we just formulated.

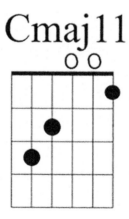

Cmaj11

- *Major 13th Chord*

Lastly, let's construct a major 13th chord. We will still be using a C to construct this chord because it is easiest to wrap your head around. As you already know, we need first to identify the root note, and in this case, C is the root note. So, the following applies:

$$C - D - E - F - G - A - B - C - D - E - F - G$$

$$1 - 2 - 3 - 4 - 5 - 6 - 7 - 8 - 9 - 10 - 11 - 12$$

With that being said, what we need to do next is to note the formula for writing a major 13th chord then apply it. The formula for writing a major 13th chord is:

$$1 - 3 - 5 - 7 - 9 - 11 - 13$$

Applying this formula to write a C major 13th chord would mean that we would have the C, E, G, B, D, F, and A notes in a C major 13th chord. But in reality, there are only six-strings on the guitar, making it impossible to have seven notes on a chord. In this case, certain notes are omitted, such as the G, F, and D notes are omitted as they can easily be played on other instruments. As such, the diagram below of a C major 13th chord makes sense.

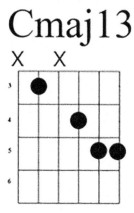

Cmaj13

Minor Chords

Just as major chords are very common in guitar playing, minor chords are no exceptions. Just as we have major triads, major 7th, and the rest, we also have minor chords in the same manner. Below is how you construct minor chords.

- ***Minor Triad Chords***

Minor triads are chords with three notes in them. To construct a minor triad chord, you need a root chord. Let us consider D as the root chord. Before we construct the chord, let's look at the scale and number:

D – E – F#/Gb – G – A – B – C#/Db

1 – 2 – 3 – 4 – 5 – 6 – 7

From the above, what you need next is the formula for constructing a minor triad chord. The formula for writing a minor triad chord is:

$1 - 3b - 5$

Now that we have all we need from the formula and scale, we can write the chord. A D minor chord has the notes D, F, and A. If you noticed, the third note was supposed to have an accidental, but the formula cancels out the accidental making it a natural. Below is what a D minor chord looks like.

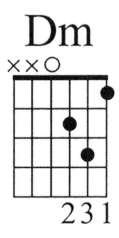

- *Minor 7th Chords*

Another type of minor chord you will come across while learning new chords on the guitar is the minor 7th chord. Let us take an example with the D minor 7th chord. Since it is a D chord, the root note is a D. As such; we will be using a D scale, meaning the following will apply:

D – E – F#/Gb – G – A – B – C#/Db – D – E – F#/Gb

1 – 2 – 3 – 4 – 5 – 6 – 7 – 8 – 9 – 10

From the number of the scale above, all we need now is the formula for writing a minor 7th chord. The formula for writing a minor 7th chord is as follows:

1 – 3b – 5 – 7b

With the analogy above, we can easily tell now that the notes you can find in a D major 7th chord are D, F, A, and C. Below is a diagram of a D major 7th chord. You can check out other D major 7th chords and compare the notes in your free time.

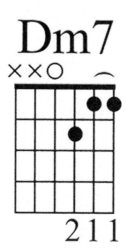

- **_Minor 9th Chords_**

The minor 9th chords are a little bit more technical. Let us stick to the simpler scale, the C scale. To write out a C minor 9th chord, you'll need to write out the C minor scale, number it, and then apply it for writing a minor 9th chord. The numbering of a C minor chord is as follows:

$$C - D - E - F - G - A - B - C - D - E$$

$$1 - 2 - 3 - 4 - 5 - 6 - 7 - 8 - 9 - 10$$

With that being said, what we need now is the formula for writing a minor 9th chord. The formula for writing a minor 9th chord is as follows:

$$1 - 3b - 5 - 7b - 9$$

Applying this formula tells us that there are five notes on a C minor 9th chord, namely C, Eb, G, Bb, and D notes. Below is a diagram of the C minor 9th chord that confirms these notes to be true.

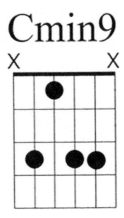

- *Minor 11th Chords*

Another minor chord we are going to be looking at is the minor 11th chords. Let us look at the C minor 11th chord, for example. Since it is a C chord, then C is the root note, so we will still be sticking to the C minor scale.

$$C - D - E - F - G - A - B - C - D - E - F - G$$

$$1 - 2 - 3 - 4 - 5 - 6 - 7 - 8 - 9 - 10 - 11 - 12$$

From the analogy above, all we need is the formula for writing a minor 11th chord, and we are good to go. The formula for writing a minor 11th chord is as follows:

$$1 - 3b - 5 - 7b - 9 - 11$$

As such, we can tell using this formula that a C minor 11th chord has six notes, namely C, D#/Eb, G, A#/Bb, D, and F. Below is a diagram confirming the notes in a C minor 11th chord. Similarly, you can check out other notes.

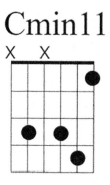

Cmin11

- *Minor 13th Chords*

Lastly, let us take a look at how the minor 13th chords are built. Let us take a look at how the C minor 13th note is being formed. The first thing we should always take note of is the root note. In this case, the root note is C, and the following applies:

$$C - D - E - F - G - A - B - C - D - E - F - G - A - B$$

$$1 - 2 - 3 - 4 - 5 - 6 - 7 - 8 - 9 - 10 - 11 - 12 - 13 - 14$$

From the above, what we need next is the formula for writing minor 13th chords. The formula for writing minor 13th chords is:

$$1 - 3b - 5 - 7b - 13$$

In other words, the notes you'll find in a C minor 13th chords are C, D#/Eb, G, A#/Bb, and A. Below is a diagram of a C minor 13th chord you can use as a reference to confirm the notes.

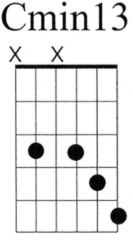

Formation of Other Complex Chords

There are not only major and minor chords on the guitar. The basics of forming any guitar chord are to know the root chord, then device the scale, writing it according to the Nashville number system. Apply the chord formula to get the notes of the chord, and you are good to go. In this section, consider it a kind of practical section where you'd have to apply yourself. We will only be introducing you to the formula of these new types of chords, and list one or two examples. What you are to do is to understand the formula and draw the chord yourself. You can also try out these chords with any scale of your choice provided you follow the instruction.

Dominant Chords

There are four main types of dominant chords we will be talking about here, namely:

1. Dominant 7th chords: The formula for writing these chords is $1 - 3 - 5 - 7b$. Common examples include G7, C7, and A7, etc.

2. Dominant 9th chords: The formula for writing these chords is $1 - 3 - 5 - 7b - 9$. Common examples include C9, D9, G9, and E9, etc.

3. Dominant 11th chords: The formula for writing these chords is $1 - 3 - 5 - 7b - 9 - 11$. Common examples include C11, D11, etc.

4. Dominant 13th chords: The formula for writing these chords is $1 - 3 - 5 - 7b - 9 - 11 - 13$. Common examples include C13 and D13, etc.

Add Chords

There are two main types of add chords we will be talking about here, namely:

1. Add 9th chords: The formula for writing these chords is $1 - 3 - 5 - 9$. Common examples include Cadd9 and Eadd9, etc.

2. Add 11th chords: The formula for writing these chords is $1 - 3 - 5 - 11$. Common examples include Cadd11, Eadd9 etc.

Sus Chords

There are two main types of Sus chords we will be talking about here, namely:

1. Sus2 chords: The formula for writing these chords is $1 - 2 - 5$. Common examples include Csus2, Esus2, etc.

2. Sus4 chords: The formula for writing these chords is $1 - 4 - 5$. Common examples include Csus4, Esus4, etc.

Altered Chords

There are four main types of altered chords we will be talking about here, namely:

1. Dominant 7th sharp 9th chords: The formula for writing these chords is $1 - 3 - 5 - 7b - 9\#$. Common examples include G7#9, E7#9, etc.

2. Dominant 7th flat 9th chords: The formula for writing these chords is $1 - 3 - 5 - 7b - 9b$. Common examples include C7b9, D7b9, etc.

3. Dominant 7th sharp 5th chords: The formula for writing these chords is $1 - 3 - 5 - 7b - 5\#$. Common examples include C7#5, A7#5, etc.

4. Dominant 7th flat 5th chords: The formula for writing these chords is $1 - 3 - 5 - 7b - 5b$. Common examples include C7b5, A7b5, etc.

Diminished Chords

There are two main types of diminished chords we will be talking about here, namely:

1. Diminished chords: The formula for writing these chords is $1 - 3b - 5b$. Common examples include Bdim, Ddim, etc.

2. Diminished 7th chords: The formula for writing these chords is $1 - 3b - 5b - 7bb$. Common examples include Cdim7, Adim7, etc.

Augmented Chords

Lastly, there are two main types of augmented chords we will be talking about here, namely:

1. Augmented chords: The formula for writing these chords is 1 – 3 – 5#. Common examples include Caug, Aaug, etc.

Augmented 7th chords: The formula for writing these chords is 1 – 3 – 5# - 7b. Common examples include Caug7, Aaug7, etc.

Chapter 10

Rhythm Techniques

So far, so good; we have been able to talk about chords on the guitar in general. So, by now, you should be quite sure of what chords mean, what notes means, and different ways to combine notes to form a chord. In this section, we will be focusing more on the topic of rhythm. Rhythm on the guitar is produced with the right hand by the action of striking strings. The pattern in which you strike the string has the greatest impact on your rhythm. While we tell every beginner to strum the guitar in a way that feels natural to what they are singing, there are different ways you can strum the guitar.

To begin, you can choose to create a rhythm with the guitar by picking the strings individually rather than striking them all at ones, especially in classical music. Also, if you're more of a rock-and-roll kind of a person, there are other strumming patterns you can indulge in that will suit the genre of music you love, like in a case where you strike all the strings with upward and downwards strokes. All these will be treated in this chapter and more. But to begin, let us first understand strumming means and the different patterns.

Strumming with Your Right Hand

Strumming is defined as dragging a pick (or your fingers) across the strings of the guitar. You can drag the pick or your finger downwards to play the chords which you fingered on the fretboard with your left hand. In doing even that, however, you create rhythm. For instance, if all you do is adhere to a tempo, or you pick-drag in a regular pattern, or even stroke, like one stroke per beat, then you are strumming the guitar in rhythm. And in reality, that's all to music, whether you are doing it intentionally or unintentionally.

To be more specific, you can strum the rhythm of a quarter-note, which is fine for some music like "Let It Be" by the Beatles or other ballads. Strumming one bar of a quarter E note looks like the notation in the diagram below, which makes use of rhythm slashes telling you to strike the enter chord rather than note heads.

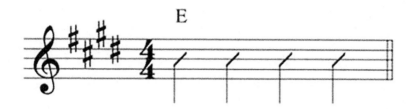

One hard part of learning guitar playing is being aware of the rhythm you are playing and still maintaining all the repetition involved. Strumming a guitar goes beyond simply striking the strings. To be able to come up with a really cool lick or riff on the guitar, you need to be consistent in your practice, have the skill, and a good understanding of musicianship.

The idea of developing a good rhythm starts from learning how to play consistently for a while, after which you can then deviate from the strumming pattern into something you cook up. The main point is to come up with something tasteful, appropriate, and not too numerous.

- ***Downstrokes***

On the staff, downstrokes are represented by a symbol that looks like an "n." Downstrokes is a type of strumming motion where you drag the pick or finger across the guitar's multiple strings. As a beginner, downstrokes are among the first types of strumming patterns to learn on a guitar because they are very basic and easy to wrap your fingers around. It is good to be consistent with downstrokes before you change from one chord to another. When playing downstrokes, you can strike all the strikes simultaneously as in strumming the strikes or plucking a string or a couple of strings at a time as in fingerpicking.

- ***Strumming Eight-Note Downstrokes***

If you want to get the most out of strumming strings, it helps to place your interest from plodding rhythms of a quarter-note strumming pattern to eighth notes. If we are to look at it mathematically, an eight-note has 1 ½ the value of a quarter note, but in music, an eight-note is twice as fast, precise, and twice as frequent. So, instead of playing a strum to a beat, you can play two strums to a beat. In other words, you will have to strike the strings two times per beat, making you move your hand twice as fast. If it were a quarter note, your hands will only be moving once per beat.

You can easily perform downstrokes on eight notes at a much moderate and slower tempo, but for a faster tempo, you may have to alternate strumming an eight-note with upstrokes and downstrokes. Below is a diagram showing you some chords and how to use the eight-note strumming pattern for each bar's first three beats and a quarter for the last beat of each bar. At the end of each bar and at the beginning of a new bar, the quarter note gives you a bit more time to switch from one chord to another. In the diagram, you will see the term sim.; it is a music notation that tells you to continue similarly. Sim is a notation used for articulation direction, such as upstrokes and downstrokes.

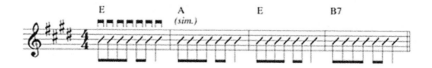

• Reading Eight-Note Downstrokes

Note, rather than using the usual slashed; we resort to slashes with stems (vertical lines drawn from the note heads) and beams (horizontal lines connecting the stems). For example, eight notes have stems and beams connecting them, which quarter notes have a single stem attached to each of them. An eight-note on its own has a little flag and not a beam.

So, even though this newly introduced notation explains specific rhythmic values such as eighth notes and quarter notes, the note heads are still angled and elongated, not in the same fashion as rounded, smaller note heads used to indicate individual pitches.

• Upstrokes

On the staff, upstrokes are represented by a symbol that looks like a "v," producing a sound opposite to that produced by downstrokes. The upstroke is a case where you drag your fingers or pick upward across the strings from the floor towards the ceiling. Playing upstrokes may see less natural than playing downstrokes, but you will eventually wrap your hands around it in no time. Another reason upstroke does not feel natural to play for beginners is because they are going against gravity. For some beginners, their challenge is in holding the pick properly, as it will occasionally get stuck between the strings.

Upstrokes are particularly useful in playing the upbeats in eight-note as the strokes in between the quarter note beats. Remember, when you start playing, don't worry yourself too much about striking all the strings in your upstroke. For instance, when you are playing an E chord with an upstroke, you don't need to strike all six strings down to the low E. Generally, your target strings should always be the first three or four strings from the bottom string or high E string.

Another thing you should note about upstrokes is that they don't get equal time as downstroke. Most times, you play the upstroke only in conjunction with downstrokes. While you can use downstroke on its own and they will sound just fine for the entire song. It is very rare to find the use of upstroke alone or without surrounding them with downstrokes.

- *Mixing Single Notes and Strum*

You can take so many more approaches to add rhythm to what you are playing on your guitar, apart from simultaneously strumming multiple strings on the guitar. Just like a piano player does not always plunk down all of his/her fingers at one to play a chord; similarly, a guitarist doesn't have to strike all the strings every time. A guitarist can pick down on single notes on the guitar to play something rhythmical.

- ***The Pick Strum***

This technique is borrowed from the piano-plunking counterpart. This method of adding rhythm to your guitar playing involves you plucking individual strings rather than strumming them. When you separate a chord into individual notes and play them, maybe the chord's base notes, it is known as a pick-strum pattern.

When you separate the treble and bass notes of a chord and play them independently in time, it is a great way to add more rhythm variety. It even adds to your chordal textures. As a guitarist, you can even set up an interplay of the different parts, a treble, and a bass complementarity or counterpart.

- ***The Boom Chick***

Another simple way to accomplish a rhythm in your guitar playing is by using the boom chick pattern. This pattern is quite efficient, and it does not require you to play all the chord notes at once. As such, you can play the bass note on the boom and the rest of the notes on the chick.

Chapter 11

Adding Melody with Pentatonic Scale and Riffs

At this point in this book, with all the knowledge impacted already, you should be able to play along with certain songs. Although playing along won't necessarily mean you're an expert yet, at least you are better off than you first started. All that's left for us to do right now is to give you some helpful tips to help you make the best out of all that you now know. As such, in this chapter, we will be introducing you to the pentatonic scale and riffs.

Pretty much everything so far in this book has taught you how to hold a chord, how they are constructed, how to strum, etc.. But we haven't talked about combining chords to play something melodious. As such, in this chapter, we will be talking about adding melody to songs with the pentatonic scale and riffs.

The Pentatonic Scale

In guitar playing or music generally, the minor and major scales are the most widely used. But when you are looking for something more melodic, then scales like the pentatonic scales begin to unfold. The pentatonic scale is not just a scale, but it is widely used to make learning chord progression easier. The beauty of the scale is the way it sounds over every chord change in a key. Just by changing and following the chord progression on the pentatonic scale, you can begin to make music with it almost immediately.

As the name suggests, there are five notes in the pentatonic scale, which differ by two notes from the normal seven notes minor and major scales. As such, these missing notes create a less linear and more open sound than either the minor or major scale. Additionally, the pentatonic scale is more ambiguous, and it is a good thing because it means you will hardly hear a bad note. When we say bad notes, we are referring to notes that may be within the key, but they may not fit well with the rest of the notes. In reality, the importance of the pentatonic scale can't be emphasized enough.

5th fret   8th fret

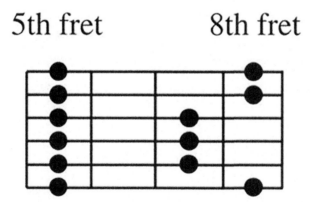

The diagram above shows the neck outline of a pentatonic scale form in the 5th position. Just like in a tab staff, the 1st string is the topmost line. Note, this is not a chord but tab staff containing the notes you can play on the pentatonic scale. All the notes on the 5th fret of the tab staff are placed with your left-hand index finger. Notes on the 7th are played using your ring finger, while notes on the 8th fret are played with your pinky finger or little finger. In this particular staff, the middle finger does not play at all.

Playing the Pentatonic Scale: Three Ways to Solo

This section will teach you how to play one pentatonic scale pattern in three different musical contexts. As a beginner, this is a trick you should have at the back of your hand as you can use it as a shortcut or quick mental calculation that allows you to wail away minor-key, major-key, or blues song. The pentatonic scale can help you get decent sounding music in virtually no time. As we get deeper into the pentatonic scale, you'd understand why its notes work the way they do.

Playing the pentatonic scale is easy when you know which finger places which note. So, to begin, place your left-hand index finger on the fifth fret of the 1st string. Ensure you relax your hand so that your other fingers don't get in the way as you play, and at the same time, they hover above the sixth, seventh, and eighth frets. In this setting, you are in the 5th position and ready to play. You can play around by working your way from the bottom to the top, playing each note singly. Don't forget to use upstrokes and downstrokes with this scale until you feel natural using it while you comfortably move your left-hand finger.

Below is a table showing the C pentatonic major in eighth notes. This particular pentatonic pattern gives your left hand a stationary position such that it allows your finger to reach their respective fret with ease without left-hand movement or stretching.

1. A Progression in a Major Key

It's time we look at the pentatonic scale in the progression of a major key. Below is a written solo of the C major in a 4/4 medium tempo grove. The solo is a mixture of eighth notes and quarter notes made up of mainly notes from the pentatonic scale of the C major, moving down and up the neck as soon as you get the idea of how the notes sound, keep practicing it until you can move from one note to the other as smoothly as you can.

2. A Progression in a Minor Key

Here is another example of the pentatonic scale in action, but the minor key. Below is a written piece in the A minor key for those who are looking for something completely different. The feel changes to a heavy backbeat 4/4 strikingly result in different sounds.

Grooving on Riffs

Riffs, on the other hand, is another component of songs like rock-and-roll used to form the perfect bridge between the melodic phrase and the chord progression. In this section, we will be venturing deep into the realms of riff playing and discovering why riffs themselves are such vital and inextricable components of rock-and-roll.

• Basic Riffs

Let us begin with the basic riff that exploits the lower register of your guitar. When playing riffs, it is important to note that striking only one string at a time, but let your pick strokes carry the same power as it will when playing chords. Even though the riff sounds familiar, it is important to execute the written piece's articulation and rhythm as precisely as possible. Make sure you do not let your ears gloss over the tricky parts.

- *Half and Whole Note Riffs*

The first thing you ought to learn about riffs is that it does not need to be flashy to be memorable. The sheet below makes use of only whole notes and half notes to create an eerie, menacing effect.

When writing a piece, you can give fretted notes with long values (whole notes and half notes) more life by applying vibrato to them with your left hand. To add vibrato, gently pull and release the string (causing a slight bending in the string) very rapidly, which causes the note to waver. With the help of vibrato in guitar playing, you can give slower notes more intensity. When you see a wavy line placed above the note, it means you should apply vibrato.

- *Eight and Quarter Note Riffs*

Another simple way to play riffs other than the slow riffs created from whole notes and half notes is the non-syncopated rhythmic unit of quarter eight and quarter notes. Below are two sheets of riffs that mix quarter notes and eight notes. So, take your time to observe the pick strike indicated for downstrokes and upstrokes.

Did you notice the F# in the key signature of both written pieces above? That means that all Fs in the written piece are sharped and that the key is neither E minor nor G major. So, even if the two riffs do not contain any Fs, we know that the examples are in E minor because the riff gravitates around the root note E.

Now, let us try out the boogie riff in the next written piece below. This boogie riff comprises mostly quarter notes, and a couple of shuffle eighth notes are thrown in to give the groove an extra kick. In the piece, the tempo is fairly bright, so be careful so that you execute the long-short rhythm of the shuffle eighth notes correctly.

A riff made of eighth notes creates a sense of continuous motion and is great in propelling a song along. Below is a piece in all eighth notes. Take note of how easily the end of the measure leads to the beginning of the second measure to create a seamless sound. Also, take note of the presence of the D# and Bb, two chromatic, or out of key, notes in E minor.

While the piece we just looked at is a simple one bar riff repeated over and over, the next piece we are about to look at below is long and steady with an eight-note phrase that goes for two measures before repeating. Because riffs are self-contained and short, they can be easily repeated back to back and looped with no break. All the riffs we looked at so far can be played seamlessly, and we encourage you to play multiple repetitions until you can play the riff flawlessly, both from the rhythmic standpoint and a technical one. The next piece we have below is a two-bar riff in steady eighth notes. You can play around with it going from one end of the riff and back to the beginning.

Remember, it is one thing to maintain a consistent and steady delivery over two bars, while it is another thing to stay solid over bars upon bars or minutes upon minutes of playing the same riff within a groove.

- *16th Note Riffs*

Lastly, let's take a look at the 16th note riffs, although they don't have to be syncopated or fast just because they have 16th notes. The piece below is a riff you can use to build up your speed as it contains quarter notes at first, then eighth notes, then 16ths.

Much heavy metal and rock riffs are based on the 16th notes, including the infamous gallop pattern. The piece below is a galloping riff you can try out on your own.

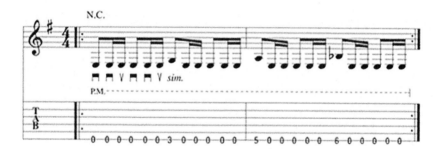

Then again, sometimes a riff written in 16th notes is going to be as fast as it can be, like in the case of hard-rock grooves in the piece below. Be sure to take note of the alternate picking indications in this example.

Chapter 12

Writing Songs and Music

At this stage, we would like first to say congratulations. Because if you followed all the steps we laid out for you so far, you should be able to play a written piece comfortably. As such, in this chapter, we will be walking you through some songs and how they are being played. Don't worry; we won't be going through the whole song, just an extract. And by the way, we will be talking about songs that use chords we treated in this chapter. In other words, you shouldn't have a problem knowing the chords or transitioning between the chords. So, without much introduction, let's just right into it.

Kumbaya

First on our list is the song Kumbaya – the ultimate campfire song. Although the origin of the song is disputable, it's an African American spiritual song. Kumbaya, meaning Come by here, is sung throughout the islands to the southern states and even the north as well. To be able to play this song, you need to be conversant with the chords A, E, and D. As for strumming, you can keep things simple by using downstrokes throughout the piece. And lastly, what you need to play this song perfectly, is to know how to make a campfire using two sticks, some dry leaves, and a magnifying glass.

Below you'll find the sheet for the song Kumbaya with all the information you'll be needing, but here are a few tips you need to take note. When playing Kumbaya, note that the pickup measure is known as the first measure. And as we know, the first measure often starts a song with a couple of missing beats. In the case of Kumbaya, it starts with the first two beats missing. Note that during the pickup measure, you should have a musical silence or rest in that part. During the musical silence, do not play anything.

Also, take note that the last bar is missing two beats in this piece – beat 3 and beat 4. As such, the missing beats in the last measure are what enable you to be able to repeat the pickup measure so you can repeat playing the song over and over again. The missing meat is what makes it possible for the measure to combine with the first incomplete one to create a total requisite of four beats.

Kumbaya

Swing Low, Sweet Chariot

Another song we will be looking at in this chapter is the all-time popular song Swing Low, Sweet Chariot. This song is an African American spiritual song referring to the Prophet Elijah's biblical story being taken to heaven by a chariot. Wallis Willis, a Choctaw freedman composed it. To play this song on the guitar, you need to be familiar with the chords D, Em, G, and A. Additionally, you'd need to have practiced your downstrokes and upstrokes as well to be able to play this piece and be able to sing like James Earl Jones.

Swing Low, Sweet Chariot starts with one beat pickup and a rest for the beat. In the sheet below, the time signature to play on is 4/4. You will also notice in the piece that beat 2 of measures 2, 4, and 6 have two strums and not one strum. So, on getting to those notes, beat a downstroke and an upstroke with each strum twice as fast as a regular strum. Don't also forget the two sharp key signatures on C and F notes, which means that any note that falls on the C or F line in the staff will be sharp.

This piece is a very easy piece to wrap your head around. Once you've got the hang of how the rhythm goes, the rest is easy peasy. Play around with this piece until you can play it as smoothly as possible. Your focus should be mainly on transitioning between the chords, so you don't abruptly pause every time you want to switch chords.

Swing Low, Sweet Chariot

Auld Lang Syne

Next, we will be looking at yet another great music piece from Auld Lang Syne. This piece is more or less a Scottish poem written by Robert Burns in the late 1780s. Auld Lang Syne was set to the tune of a traditional folk song "Roud." In many countries, this piece was used to bid farewell to the old years at the stroke of midnight on New Year's Eve. To play this piece, you need to be able to play the chords Em, D, C, Am, and G. And for the rhythm, you need to be able to play down and down-up strums on the guitar.

This piece is a bit longer than other pieces we have been treating so far, so it might require a bit of more attention and time to wrap your head around. But one thing is sure; this piece is something you can play on the guitar because you have been taught everything you need to know about playing this piece. However, measure 8 in this piece is a little tricky because you will have to play three different chords in that same measure. In measure 8, you will have to play the D, Am, and Em in the same measure.

Note, you'd have to change chord on each beat when you move to the second half of the measure, i.e., one strike per chord. You can start by playing measure 8 slowly, repeatedly. And in no time, you'd see yourself playing the whole song effortlessly. Take note, when changing from G to C, (bars 4-6 and 12-19), fingering G with fingers 2, 3, and 4 instead of 1, 2, and 3 make the chord switch easier. The third and second fingers form a shape that simply moves one string.

Auld Lang Syne

Michael, Row the Boat Ashore

Another song you can play using basic major and minor chords is this song Michael, Row the Boat Ashore, an African-American spiritual song first noted during the American Civil War at St. Helena Island. The best-known recording of this folk music was released in 1960 by the U.S. bank The Highwaymen. Today, this song is sung all over the world. To play this song, you need to be able to play the chords G, F, Em, Dm, and C chords and how to play a syncopated eighth-note strum.

Before you begin, it would be best if you took your time to look through the sheet and understand the time signature, strumming pattern, and every other piece of information embedded in the sheet. For this sheet, you'd need to be conversant with downstrokes and upstrokes as well as a sim. The strumming pattern in this song is syncopated. So, the strum that usually occurs on beat 3 is anticipated; it comes half a beat early. This kind of strumming pattern gives the song a Latin feel. Take note of the 4/4-time signature as well, when playing this song.

Michael, Row the Boat Ashore

Home on the Range

So far, so good; we have looked at a couple of songs you can play using the basic major and minor chords. Now, let us look at songs that involve a little bit of the seventh chords. Below is a sheet on how to play the classical western folk song, Home on the Range, sometimes called the American West's unofficial anthem. This song is pretty straightforward, although it is a bit long, it involves simple chords you already know. To play this song, you need to be conversant with the chords G7, D7, F, C7, and C. You also need to know how to play a bass strum pattern, and for fun, how to wail like a coyote.

There are a few things to note about the sheet, especially the strumming pattern. In the sheet, you bass strum over the rhythm slashes, rather than simply strumming the chord for three beats, play only the lowest notes of the chords starting from the first beat and then strum the remaining notes of the chord on the second and third beat. The sim in this sheet means you should keep playing this pattern throughout the sheet.

Home on the Range

All Through the Night

In conclusion, let us take a look at one more song you can play involving the seventh chords. Jules Shear originally recorded all Through the Night. This song is a mid-tempo folk-rock song you can groove on when you feel like hearing something somnolent. To play this song, you need to be able to play the chords A7, E7, G, and D. You also need to know how to repeat signs. For the E7 in this track, use the two fingers variant, it makes it easy to switch between chords.

In the sheet below, the repeat signs (two dots that look like a colon) means you will play a certain measure twice. As such, you are to play measures 1, 2, 3, 4, and then measures 1, 2, 3, 5 twice.

All Through the Night

Chapter 13

Ten Common Guitar Mistakes to Avoid

L astly, in this chapter, let's go through how to improve your playing skills. Because at this stage, we have practically taught you everything you need to know as a beginner. All that's left for you to do right now is to practice, practice and practice. And as you practice, make sure you try out something new every time. Because to be real with you, learning the guitar is very vast and takes a lot of time and patience. Plus, you can easily be making one mistake or the other as you learn. So, we came up with this chapter to enlighten you on some common bad habits you might be picking up as you learn. It's better to learn how to play the guitar the right way from the start rather than having to correct bad habits later on as you advance. With that being said, here are ten mistakes you should not make.

1. *Playing with Too Much Effort*

While you need quite an amount of energy to firmly hold the chord, your fingers need to be flexible. It might take a little bit of practicing from you before you can get your hands around holding strings firmly such that they are still flexible to switch between notes easily. Many beginners make that mistake of stiffening their fingers way too much when holding notes. Then after playing the note, they find it difficult to switch to another note quickly without pausing. This pause to switch to another note will affect your sound and make what you're playing not enjoyable. And the worst part about applying too much effort with your fingers will lead to early fatigue. You may even begin to feel pains way too early than you should, thereby shortening the amount of time you can practice, which slows down your overall progress.

2. Learning with a Low-Quality Guitar

Another thing you should be mindful of is not getting a professional guitar setup. Much of what we just explained about using too much effort to play all comes down to getting a good instrument that's easy to play. When the guitar you purchased isn't professional, it may lead you to believe you need to use so much effort on the strings for them to sound right. Very often, a low-quality guitar has higher strings actions that require you to use more effort to press the string. No matter how little the difference is between the string and the fretboard, it will be felt by the fingers even if it is in millimeters. The main thing a professional guitar offers you is the lower string action. Not to even mention the sounds of the low-quality guitar as they are usually off. Don't allow the guitar price to push you to get a guitar you'd later regret buying or a guitar that will make learning such a headache for you.

3. Learning Too Fast

While you may want to go as fast as you can to show you're a skilled guitarist, it's alright to take things slow as a beginner. After learning the notes you're to use to play a song, it's alright if you can't follow the song at 100% speed as a beginner. Instead, try to bring the song's tempo to about 50% to give you time to switch between chords. Because as a beginner, one of the major struggles is in switching chords. And you must know that it's alright if you're slow when switching between chords; eventually, your speed will increase. What matters is that you keep at it, be consistent, and eventually, you'll feel that there is a gradual increase in your playing speed. As a beginner, don't make the mistake of trying to practice high tempo songs. Go for songs with a slow tempo. Also, it's important you avoid sloppy practices while switching chords.

4. *Not Using a Metronome to Practice*

We just talked about taking things slowly; to achieve that properly, you need a metronome. The metronome is a very versatile tool that comes in handy when you're practicing a song. The metronome helps you achieve three main things: Firstly, you can use it to slow down your practice. Secondly, you can use the metronome to build a natural sense of rhyme. And thirdly, you can use the metronome to get a clear idea of the progression you're practicing. No doubt, it's easier to practice at a slower pace, but most people tend to start practicing a song slowly, then unknowingly speed up down the line. This often happens when you practice without a metronome. But if you practice with a metronome, it counters this effect by giving you a clear indicator to follow. Because if you slow down too much or speed up, the metronome will let you know.

5. *Using Too Many Effects to Practice*

While it might sound great to add vibrato, riffs, and reverb to whatever song you're playing, too much of it is always bad. We're not trying to discourage you or say you should not practice with effects; on the contrary, effects help you cover up sloppy techniques and mistakes, but try to keep the use of effects to average. You can split your practice session into two sessions, where you practice with effects in one session, and your practice without effects in the other session. This way, you'll be able to evaluate your techniques without a wash of sound covering your mistakes.

6. *Inconsistent Practice*

One major bad habit you should avoid is not being consistent in your practice. Practicing once a month will have little to no effect on your playing ability. If you truly want to learn how to play the guitar, set aside a certain time of the day and days of the week, you will be free to practice. The more you practice, the more you have what is called muscle memory. Practicing the guitar involves a lot of complex motor skills. The best way you can make these movements seem effortless and natural is by consistent repetition, which comes down to practice. It's better to practice for 1 hour every day than for 10 hours on a single day. The key to muscle memory is consistency.

7. *Not Learning Music Theory*

As a beginner, you should not think of learning music theory as too much trouble. Although music theory can be quite technical at first glance, in reality, they are not, especially when you spend some time to understand it. In fact, they are even quite fascinating and interesting. Having a good understanding of music theory widens your knowledge of how best to combine chords and how to transition from one key to another, among many other great advantages. No doubt, learning music theory may be time consuming, they are definitely worth every second of your time. Without a good background in music theory, you'll simply just be memorizing scale shapes and chord progressions. Think of it as a formula for improving your understanding of the guitar without having to memorize so much.

8. *Trying to Learn Too Much at Once*

While we've taught you so many things in this book, it's advisable not to gulp everything at once. So, take your time to digest them one at a time. The time you spend getting yourself acquainted and able to play a particular lesson effortlessly does not matter; what truly matters is that you're able to do it. But don't confuse this to think being highly motivated to learn more is bad. The issue is in moving to learn something new, before even mastering the song you were previously learning. Learning all the modes in 12 keys and all the scale shapes is a great objective, especially if you can work hard and be disciplined enough to learn them all. But it is best if you focus on one or two things rather than to be mediocre at everything.

9. *Not Learning Other Genres of Music*

You may not quickly pick up on this error, but limiting yourself to one music genre isn't a great way to learn. Although learning how to play a genre of music you love helps make learning enjoyable, don't limit yourself to just one music genre. Every piece of music has something it will teach you in your playing skills. Additionally, when you start listening to other music genres, you'd be surprised at how much inspiration from different chord combinations and rhythms will be coming to you. For example, if you listen to rock a lot, you'd be quite conversant with strumming patterns, but when you start listening to blues and classical music, you will get to understand more about fingerpicking.

10. Obsession with Perfection

Lastly, getting too caught up with perfection is another common error of a lot of beginners, especially within the early stages of practice. Everyone sounds unique and different because we all have our quirks. So, rather than trying to be so perfect, it's alright to have a little quirk in your sound. So, don't get all worked up or disappointed anytime you hear an irregularity in your sound as you learn. This doesn't mean you shouldn't try your best to practice perfectly to get the best result in perfect technique. We are trying to say that you should focus on getting everything as perfect as you can when you're performing and learn to turn off that inner critic and just play.

Conclusion

To sum things up, while learning new things on the guitar helps you play better, practice is the key to becoming an expert. You need to be consistent with your practice, as we have been emphasizing. And if you truly want to enjoy learning the guitar, it is always a great idea to invest some money in getting a high-quality guitar. With a high-quality guitar, you won't have to stress so much to get the best sound from the guitar. As such, your fingers won't hurt so much, letting you play for a longer period.

We've talked about how to buy a guitar. Use the information we provided as a guide to educate yourself on what you need to keep in mind when shopping for the best guitar. Remember, when getting a guitar, try not to be too focused on the price. While you may have a budget, your aim should be in getting the best guitar, and not the cheapest guitar you can lay your hands on. And after buying a guitar, ensure you string it with the right string that suits you. Plus, tuning the guitar can be a bit of a pain, but we talked about different ways to tune the guitar, so you can use any one of them that you felt comfortable with.

Also, take note of the basic playing strategies we talked about; one is to learn the beginner's chord first before moving to the more technical ones later on. As a beginner learning how to play the guitar, your major struggle may be with switching between chords. If you experience this struggle, do not be discouraged. Struggling with switching between chords is common amongst beginners. It helps to start off as slow as it feels convenient for you. Work on improving your speed by practicing consistently.

The best way to learn how to play the guitar is by playing along with your favorite songs. Since you know the song, you won't have a problem with coping with the rhythm. Most importantly, all you need to know is the chord progression and perhaps the strumming pattern; you can then play any song. Practicing with your favorite song makes guitar learning fun.

Printed in Great Britain
by Amazon